Success as an Online Student

This book is dedicated to the many hardworking students who sacrifice family time to better themselves; to the many teachers who light the way for their students; and to our own families, who understand better than anyone why we teach.

Success as an Online Student
Strategies for Effective Learning

Kevin J. Fandl
Jamie D. Smith

Routledge
Taylor & Francis Group

LONDON AND NEW YORK

First published 2013 by Anderson Publishing

Published 2015 by Routledge
2 Park Square, Milton Park, Abingdon, Oxon OX14 4RN

and by Routledge
711 Third Avenue, New York, NY 10017, USA

Routlege is an imprint of the Taylor & Francis Group, an informa business

British Library Cataloguing-in-Publication Data
A catalogue record for this book is available from the British Library

Library of Congress Cataloging-in-Publication Data
A catalog record for this book is available from the Library of Congress

ISBN 978-1-4557-7632-0 (pbk)

CONTENTS

PREFACE

Online university learners face two significant challenges that most traditional university students do not: they usually have full- or part-time jobs and families to care for while they study; and, on top of that, they usually lack access to a traditional learning environment with the kind of interaction and social bonding found in traditional schools. However, many online students also exhibit extraordinary drive and motivation to succeed. That is why they sought out online education in the first place. These students recognize, perhaps more than a traditional university student, the value of their education and the benefits of making an investment of time and money to secure a better future for themselves and their families.

This book is a practical guide for anyone considering, or already a part of, the online education process. This book will help anyone who is considering their first online class, anyone currently enrolled in an online class who wants to maximize his or her return from online education, and anyone approaching graduation or just entering the job market with a degree earned online. The authors, seasoned professionals with substantial online teaching and learning experience, deliver concise guidance to make the online learning journey enjoyable, productive, and most of all, worthwhile. This includes discussions of the traits of successful online students, tips for excelling in online classes, strategies to enhance marketability after graduation, and recommendations for achieving work–life–family balance, managing stress, and applying effective time management to your studies and life. As the singular guide to success as an online learner, this practical book aims to be the compendium to anyone considering enrolling in an online class or who wants to gain the knowledge they need to succeed as an online student.

ABOUT THE AUTHORS

Kevin J. Fandl is a legal writing and legal English scholar with extensive publishing and teaching experience. He served as a managing editor for the *Foreign Policy Bulletin* for 3 years and as a senior editor of the *American University International Law Review* for 2 years. He has published ten law review articles, several editorials and book reviews, and three books on law and legal writing. He is the director of the Global Legal Education Institute, which develops and delivers on-site training around the world on numerous US law topics, including legal English and legal writing. Dr. Fandl earned his master's degree in international relations, his Juris Doctor degree in law from American University, and his doctorate in public policy from George Mason University. He lectures frequently at the Georgetown University Law Center and the American University Washington College of Law, and consults for the World Bank and the Organization of American States. He has taught online at numerous universities since 2004.

Jamie D. Smith is an attorney who has been teaching since 2006 and teaching online since 2007. During this time she has taught in numerous undergraduate and graduate programs. She is a full-time faculty member at an online university and has previously served as chair of an online program. Jamie received her Juris Doctor degree and a master's degree in international affairs with a concentration in international law and organizations from the George Washington University. Smith is licensed to practice law in the District of Columbia, has extensive civil litigation and appellate experience, and is a certified mediator.

INTRODUCTION

An investment in knowledge pays the best interest.[1]

—Benjamin Franklin

Laurie always dreamed of going to college, but with a young child and a full-time job she wasn't sure how she could ever achieve her dream. One day, while thinking about how she could position herself to get a promotion at work, she started researching online schools. She found one that was a perfect fit for her and now, just a few years later, she is sitting behind the manager's desk.

By reading this book you have taken the first step toward ensuring a brighter future for yourself and your family. Deciding whether to enroll in an online program is a big decision that will require a lot of hard work and dedication. You are doing the right thing by reading this book to make sure that you choose the best program for you and to ensure that you are prepared to succeed in that program.

Whether you are still deciding on a program to enroll in or you are approaching graduation, we know that attending school is not easy. We have been teaching online and balancing our own families and full-time jobs for almost 10 years. And we have both been students at a number of different schools on our own paths to success. We know that you are struggling and overwhelmed and possibly even a little frightened of what to expect and whether you can handle the demands that come along with taking classes online. That is precisely why we wrote this book. This is not a book that offers you theories for success or a ranking of online universities to pick from. Rather, it is a practical toolkit based on years of teaching and learning experience in traditional and online environments, which will steer you in the right direction toward your educational goals. In addition to our teaching experience, we have both been in positions where we have supervised and hired employees—we know what makes the best employees. We draw on this

---

[1]Benjamin Franklin, Poor Richard's Almanac.

experience to help you maximize your time in school to give you the best chance of getting your dream job once you graduate.

Education is the most valuable investment that you can make in yourself. Education will not only expand your knowledge—it will open doors to job opportunities, increase your marketability, and enhance your ability to communicate as a professional in your field. Your decision to enroll in an academic program, whether traditional, hybrid, or online, is an indication that you recognize the value of education and that you are ready to make an investment in yourself—an investment that will pay great dividends for you and your family.

Despite the substantial number of traditional colleges and universities spread around the country, some individuals who want to realize their educational dream don't have access to a traditional program that is the right fit for them. Many of these individuals live in areas where, although there may be schools, those schools don't offer programs that the individual desires or a schedule that works for them. A nearby college that offers a range of paralegal programs will not help the individual interested in learning about how to open his or her own business. A nearby university that offers business classes only during the day will not help the individual who needs to keep her nine-to-five job while in school. Other individuals do not have access to traditional colleges or universities at all because they live or work overseas, either because they serve in the armed forces or simply because they moved abroad as a work or life choice. Still others are unable to commute to a traditional university due to distance, time, or cost. For these individuals, online education can provide access to the program that they want no matter where they live.

One barrier that some potential students may face to enrolling in school is a lack of time to complete their education. In a traditional model, a student lives on or commutes to a campus and takes a series of classes, often spread throughout the daytime hours. If a student at a traditional school holds a job, it is usually a part-time job and often allows them to work evening hours and allows them to plan their schedule around their classes. But for many individuals, a schedule like this is impossible. This may be due to a full-time work schedule, daytime working hours, or family responsibilities, among other things. For these individuals, online education can provide flexibility in attending classes regardless of other commitments.

Online education is not for everyone. If your goal is to leave home and move to a college town, where you will have an opportunity to live in dormitories, eat at the campus cafeteria, take live classes, and socialize with hundreds of other students, a traditional college or university may be a better fit for you. Yet even these traditional universities are beginning to see the benefits of online education and have shifted some of their classes to the online learning environment.[2] As higher education makes this transition toward more flexible and accessible classes, you will be presented with numerous learning opportunities, regardless of your field of interest. You will be presented with opportunities to socialize and network as well.

Deciding that you want to enroll in an online academic program is only the first step on your journey. You still need to determine which school to attend, in which field you will pursue your studies, with what type of degree or certificate you want to graduate, if any, and how much time and money you are willing to invest to achieve your goals. We will discuss how to select the right field and degree in-depth in this book, but first we will talk briefly about your time and money investment, because finding the right program will not do you much good if you cannot make these necessary investments.

TURNING YOUR PENNIES INTO GOLD

An online educational program, much like a traditional program, is meant to be rigorous and intense. In some cases, you may even find online classes require more of your time and attention than a live class at a traditional university would because they may operate on an accelerated schedule. The key distinction, of course, is that you decide when to invest that time, whether on a weekend, after work, or in the early morning hours. But it would be incorrect to assume that because a course is being offered online it is any less rigorous than a live course. Before you enroll in an online program, make sure that you are prepared for the work that is involved.

Education is also an investment in money. For most potential students, the decision to attend school represents an investment in their future. The cost of online programs vary widely, depending on the

[2]For example, Harvard University offers over 600 online classes as of the time of this publication. http://www.extension.harvard.edu/

type of degree sought, the length of the program, and the reputation of the school. One factor in your decision of whether and where to attend school should be the cost of your education. Loans may be available to help you finance the cost of an education. After completing your education you will be in a more competitive position to earn a higher salary. Hopefully, your increased earnings will more than offset the investment you made in your education. Scholarships, grants, and money available through a variety of programs, such as the Veterans Bill of Rights, may help to fund your education. Many employers also offer tuition assistance because they recognize the value of well-educated employees who can make greater contributions to the organization. However, most students take some loans to fund their education and you must be prepared to begin paying back your loans within months of graduation. Admissions counselors and financial aid consultants at the school you would like to attend can help you navigate through this process and help you obtain the funding you need.

In this book, we will introduce you to the world of online learning by telling you about its benefits and drawbacks and how it differs from traditional educational programs. We will give you advice on selecting a program, if you haven't already enrolled, and recommendations for enhancing your online experience once you begin your program. All of these fundamentals are contained in the first section of this book.

In the second section, we will guide you through a number of hurdles that may prevent you from achieving your educational goals. This includes a chapter on time management with a typical online student in mind; finding a work/life balance to keep your family intact and happy while you achieve your goals; and a chapter each on effective research strategies and writing tips to help you excel in all of your classes and rise above your classmates. You will find everything you need to not just make your online learning experience possible, but enjoyable, rewarding, and most importantly successful.

In the final section of the book, we will help you strategize for success after you graduate. You may not be thinking quite yet about that day (or you may already be counting down to that day), but it is wise to prepare yourself as early as possible. This section offers tips for networking with your colleagues and professors starting as early as your first substantive class. It provides tips for preparing yourself for a job after graduation (hint: you need more than a degree to get the job!). And it provides recommendations for continuing to advance your own professional development once you graduate. You will find this section to be uplifting and practical and we encourage you to read it before you get too far along in your program.

So, with this introduction, we welcome you to your online learning experience and wish you great success. Remember that our success as professors, and the success of a college or university, depends almost entirely on your success. So, for our sake, as well as your own, jump in and do a great job!

Considering Online Education

CHAPTER 1

Choosing an Online School and Program

Alan has made the decision to enroll in an online program because he knows it is the best way to get ahead. He talks to some friends who have taken classes online but doesn't think that programs that worked for them are right for him. To help him find a program that fits his lifestyle and aspirations, Alan carefully considers how much time he can devote to school and his future job goals. After doing some research, he finds a program that is a perfect fit and goes on to graduate with honors.

1.1 INTRODUCTION

Online universities offer many advantages whether you are an 18-year-old recent high school graduate considering college, a 30-something needing a fresh start, or a 60-year-old retiree looking to learn something new. Online classes offer the convenience of classes that you can take at home or on the road. They offer the flexibility of taking classes anytime of day or night, allowing you to work, manage family obligations, and keep your routines while still fitting in classes. And they offer a broad variety of programs from criminal justice, to paralegal studies, to public policy, to IT, to nursing, and on and on. The possibilities for your future are nearly unlimited.

But once you have made the decision that online education is for you, how do you decide where to enroll? And how do you settle on a particular program of study? With the plethora of online universities and traditional universities offering online classes in almost every area imaginable, you don't have to limit yourself to universities in your home community. In fact, unless the school requires residency for a period of time, the only time you may even see the campus is for graduation—if you even attend that. This means that your choice of school is expansive, which makes your choice more exciting, but also more difficult.

There are plenty of ranking programs that you can look to if you want to know which schools are ranked highest for various programs.

However, these rankings are only part of the story because an online program must fit your goals and lifestyle to be the best for you. Moreover, a school that has an excellent reputation for their homeland security program may not be as strong in their teaching program. Thus, this book will not tell you which school is the best school because there is no such thing. Schools are not "one size fits all" so the school that is best for one person may not be the best for someone else. We have both taught at a number of schools and have heard stories at each one from students who love the school and students who are less satisfied. It all depends on your perspective and what you hope to attain from the program. So instead of telling you which school to attend, this book will advise you on what factors you should be looking for to ensure that the school you choose is the best match for you and for the career you want.

1.2 SELECTING A SCHOOL

There are three types of online options from which you can choose: fully online schools, traditional schools that offer online courses, and hybrid schools. Fully online schools led the revolution in education taking what used to be known as correspondence education (classes and lessons completed via mail) and combining it with many of the best features of traditional education, such as real-time interaction, access to extensive learning resources, and accreditation. More recently, traditional universities have seen the value in offering distance education programs and have either established unique divisions for online education or simply added a variety of online classes that you can combine with traditional live classes. Hybrid schools are those that primarily offer courses online but offer some live classes as part of their programs through satellite locations in various areas.

Which model you choose largely depends on your answer to the following questions:

1. How flexible is your schedule?
2. How important is live, direct interaction with a professor to you?
3. How close do you live to a traditional university?

Once you have completed reading this book, you may want to reassess your answers to these questions.

If you have little flexibility in your schedule, either because you work full-time, manage family responsibilities, travel extensively, serve in the armed forces, or what have you, online options are probably a better choice for you. Even if you live near a traditional university, your schedule may prevent you from attending every class and getting the most out of that school. You would not be able to take full advantage of the key elements that traditional schools offer and online schools do not. Thus, you would not be giving yourself the best chance for success.

If you are someone who depends on direct, in-person contact with your professors frequently, you may not appreciate the model of online universities. In a traditional school, you will have access, during office hours or scheduled appointments, to speak directly with your professors. In the online environment, you will interact on the discussion boards with your professor every day, and you will be able to e-mail them as often as you need to. You may even be able to call them to discuss your concerns. However, almost all of this will be done virtually rather than in-person. This is a trade-off that you would have to make—infrequent but live access at traditional schools or frequent but virtual access at online schools.

Finally, do you live close to a school that you would be willing and able to attend? If you do not, and assuming you would not want to move to attend school, an online university may be the best option for you. This is especially true for military families, who are often stationed overseas and may move frequently. While these families have Internet access, they do not have access to a university that they could attend in person or one that they know they could attend until they have completed their degree. This is one of the key benefits of online education, and it neatly fills the gap in areas where access to a traditional university is limited.

1.3 SOME DISTINCTIONS BETWEEN ONLINE PROGRAMS

Each online program attempts to add something unique to the educational experience. This could be a focus on a single subject area, such as law or nursing. Or it could be a unique approach to online learning, such as through video seminars or residencies. Below you will find a list of some of the major distinctions that we have seen in our experiences at a number of online schools. You may find some of them particularly appealing to your learning style and that may drive your decision on which school to choose.

- *Residencies*: Some schools (mostly graduate programs) require students to attend one or more live sessions known as residencies. These sessions allow students to come together with their classmates and several professors with whom they may have interacted with during their online courses. Students generally receive live lectures during these residencies and have one-on-one time with the professors and academic staff to help guide them through their learning process. In many cases, residencies are in interesting locations both domestically and internationally, giving students the added benefit of traveling; of course, this means additional expenses as well.
- *Mission*: Many online universities are driven by a particular mission. For some students, this is particularly important as it ensures that the school recognizes and appreciates the beliefs of the student. These missions may be religious, social, or discipline-based and are usually stated clearly on the school's web page.
- *Audio and video lectures*: Most online learning is done in what is called an asynchronous learning environment, meaning that your interactions with other students and your professor are not done in real-time. You may receive a response in minutes, depending on who is online (think of instant messaging) but most responses take several hours or even a day to be responded to. Some schools compensate for this with synchronous lectures, often weekly, where the students will either hear or see their professor deliver a lecture. This may be done using conference call lines, Adobe Connect, or a number of other platforms for live (synchronous) interaction. Bear in mind that to take full advantage of this, an excellent Internet connection and computer is required. You must also be able to attend the lecture when it is being presented. Although live lectures have some advantages, they do take away some of the flexibility of online learning. Most schools that offer live lectures will offer recorded versions to their students that you can review anytime, but you will lose the main benefit of these lectures which is the opportunity to interact in real-time with your professor and classmates.
- *Prerecorded lectures*: An alternative to synchronous lectures is a prerecorded lecture by your professor or another expert in the subject area. At some schools, you can access these lectures each week,

often accompanied by PowerPoint or similar presentations. At some schools, these lectures are not conducted by your professor. Unlike synchronous lectures, the prerecorded lectures can be listed to anytime. These lectures do not allow for live question and answer sessions that you would get with the live lectures, but keep in mind that your professor will be available to answer any questions that you have.

• *Access to live and hybrid classes*: If you are not at a fully online university, you may have the ability to take live or hybrid classes if it fits your schedule. Some traditional universities that offer online components will allow their students to enroll in any of these three types of classes. Hybrid classes are a blend of online and live teaching where you spend less time in the classroom than you would at a traditional school but you also work online with your professor and colleagues. This is ideal for students who live within a reasonable distance of where the live and hybrid classes are offered but want to take advantage of the benefits of online learning. The live component of hybrid classes may be offered at satellite locations that may not be located on the school's main campus.

• *Length and Timing of Courses*: Some schools offer courses as long as 11 weeks. Other schools offer courses as short as 5 weeks. Longer courses usually run at a slower pace than shorter courses as there is more time to cover the material. On the other hand, shorter courses may offer you more flexibility to take time off as needed to accommodate travel schedules or busy times at work. Moreover, some schools offer monthly start dates for classes, while others operate on a semester schedule with courses starting once a quarter. Flexibility in start dates may work better for some students, while the predictability of set start dates work better for others.

1.4 CHOOSING THE RIGHT PROGRAM

Sally is a big fan of CSI Miami. She dreams of one day becoming a forensics expert, engaging in exciting investigations like they do on television. She decides that she will go to school online to achieve that dream.

What we see on television or at the movies can often inspire us to do great things. Many who watch medical dramas dream of going to medical school to become a doctor. People that can't miss an episode of the latest legal thriller aspire to be criminal investigators or even prosecutors. That dream does not come true for most of us, but that doesn't discount the value of inspiration in driving our education and career choices or where that path may lead you.

However, your decision about the program in which you should enroll should not be based on that dream alone—there are also practical considerations. Consider Sally, who wants to be a forensics expert. She will likely find a long list of universities that offer programs in forensic science and criminal investigations. She could easily enroll in any one of those. However, Sally needs to think about a few other things as well before making a decision. Some things she should consider are:

1. What kind of degrees do people have in the field I want to enter?
2. What does the job market for this profession look like today? What will it look like when I graduate?
3. What skills will I learn in this program and how will they help me in my intended career?
4. Are the skills that I learn transferrable to other professions?

The first thing that you should do is learn about the career that you want to have. A simple Internet search will reveal many real people, not actors playing them on television, working in this field. Learn about their backgrounds, qualifications, and experience. If you can, reach out to them to ask them how they got to where they are today. Then, go to job sites advertising for this type of position. What qualifications do they call for? In many cases, they will tell you the types of degrees that they consider appropriate for those jobs. Does the program that you are considering match one of those? You can also research the backgrounds of professors teaching in the field. Most schools publish biographies of professors on their web sites. As most schools hire professors that are experts in their field, the backgrounds of these professors will provide insights into what it takes to be successful.

Next, consider the job market today and what it will look like in a few years for this profession. Look at those job sites again and count the number of jobs in this field for which you would be qualified upon graduation. Be sure to check their location—while online learning is possible from anywhere, most jobs still require you to be on site every day. If you dream of becoming a forest ranger, but your spouse's career will prevent you from leaving New York City, you should probably consider a different career path. Look for articles discussing trends in the profession. One of the best places to find out about trends in different fields is the US Department of Labor. You can access their list of occupational trends from this page: http://www.bls.gov/emp/. For example, according to the 2012–13 edition of their guide, job growth is most significant in the fields of personal care and healthcare. With a growing population of baby boomers in their retirement years, this makes sense. Check out this guide to see the latest job trends.

The third thing that you should consider when selecting a program of study is how the skills you will learn will prepare you for work in this field. The name of a program does not necessarily match the classes or skills that the program offers. You may find, for instance, that a school advertising for a degree in legal studies offers little in the way of actual legal training but rather prepares you to work in an administrative position at a law firm. Carefully research the types of classes you would have to take to receive your degree and assess whether those classes would give you the skills you need to succeed in your chosen field.

Finally, be aware of the variability of the job market. Even if you have selected one of the fastest-growing career tracks out there, you may still face a sudden shortage or unemployment down the road. Does your degree prepare you to work in related professions? Or if that terrible day comes when your boss eliminates your job, will you have to enroll in school again to get another degree in order to find another job? Many programs give you the flexibility to work in a number of fields. If you are too specific in your program of study, you may actually make yourself less competitive in the workplace. Remember that much of what will land you the job you want depends on your skills and experience, not the title of your degree.

Your approach to finding the right program ultimately depends on your ability to identify the type of job that you want to be qualified to take. At this stage, that job may be nebulous or uncertain, but if you can focus in on the type of job that would make you happy, whether it is as a forensics specialist or a paralegal, you can begin to identify the skills you will need to get that job. Don't be distracted by program titles or even job titles. Focus on the skills that you will need to do what you want to do. Then find the program that offers you those very skills.

1.5 CHOOSING THE BEST DEGREE

Once you have decided on the field of study and program that you are interested in studying, you need to decide how far you want to go with it. Do you want to obtain your first-level degree in this area (Bachelor's degree)? Do you already have a relevant first-level degree and instead plan on studying for a Masters or Doctoral degree? Would a certificate program be better for you? Or do you just need to take a few classes to get up to speed in your field? It is generally more affordable to study for a certificate program than for a degree, but a degree is usually given more weight by employers. Graduate school is generally more expensive than college. And an MBA or LLM is probably more expensive than an MA or MS degree. But how do you know which to pursue?

When you consider the costs of your education, take the following factors into account as you compare schools:

1. The degree that you will receive upon completion.
2. The accreditation and reputation of the school.
3. The employment prospects upon graduation.
4. The length of the program (in many cases, an accelerated program will be more expensive per semester but less expensive overall).

If you are interested in becoming a lawyer, you should look for a prelaw (undergraduate) or Juris Doctor (graduate) program rather than a paralegal or legal studies program. If you are interested in becoming a business professional, you should look for a business (undergraduate) or MBA (graduate) program rather than a program in, say, organizational management. Selecting the right degree can mean the difference between graduating once and graduating two or three times with related degrees. Look at practitioners in your field of interest and identify the degrees that they have allowed them to practice in that field. Then look for those degree programs at your schools of interest. We once had a student interested in becoming a consultant for the government. She obtained a degree in public policy only to find out after an investment of 2 years and several thousand dollars that all of the large firms required an MBA for consultant positions. With a little research upfront, you can avoid being in this situation and get the job you want.

Accreditation is discussed in an upcoming chapter. But, in addition to accreditation, you should consider the reputation of the schools to which you wish to apply. Some schools are stronger in certain areas, as measured by their job placement rates in those fields and the publications on topics within those fields. Many online universities emphasize certain subject areas and recruit top talent to teach in those areas. That is often an indication of a good reputation in that field. However, to be sure, always find out what percentage of graduates from your program of interest are employed in the first 6–12 months following graduation, and if you can, secure a list of recent employers where graduates landed jobs. Most schools will be happy to share this information as it highlights their own success.

1.6 QUALITY OF THE SCHOOL

How do you know if the school you are considering is a high-quality school? Again, you can always refer to the rankings by *US News and World Report*, among others. But what you should be most focused on with respect to online schools is the following:

1. Job placement rates—How many graduates are employed upon or within 6 months of graduation?
2. Career service programs—What assistance does the school offer to help you find a job?
3. Accreditation—Has the school been regionally accredited (discussed more below)?
4. Quality of faculty—Do faculty members have graduate degrees from accredited universities and experience in their field?
5. Class size—Are classes capped to allow for maximum interaction with professors and colleagues?

In addition to these factors, ask the recruiter or research online what kinds of positions graduates of that school have been able to obtain and how many students find employment within a year after graduation. Whether their graduates have been selected for reputable positions, either in government, in private industry, or in academia, can speak volumes about how a degree from that school is perceived by the job market. Many schools like to highlight their star performers. How many of these stars has the school had in recent years, and does it suggest a trend toward more or less high performers? Assuming that you count yourself among the star performer crowd (and hopefully you will after reading this book), you will want to be at a school that values them and helps them achieve the greatness for which they are destined.

1.7 ACCREDITATION

The final thing that you should look for in a school is accreditation. According to the American Psychological Association:

> *As a student: Accreditation provides assurance that the program in which you are enrolled or are considering enrolling is engaged in continuous review and improvement of its quality, that it meets nationally endorsed standards in the profession, and that it is accountable for achieving what it sets out to do.*[1]

The advent of online education has also led to the rise of many schools that do not meet the basic educational standards set forth by accrediting bodies. This is something that you should consider when selecting the school you plan to attend.

1.7.1 What Is Accreditation?

Accreditation refers to the review and approval process by a national, regional, or state accrediting body of a particular school. The review focuses on the quality of education provided at that institution and its ability to meet the standards set forth by that accrediting body. It is evidence that the school strives for excellence in education. Note that accreditation is a voluntary process—a school does not have to request accreditation to operate. However, accreditation does provide assurance that the school has met rigorous standards for quality and excellence and assures future employers that you attended a quality program.

1.7.2 Which Accrediting Body Matters?

Some states have accrediting bodies for universities within their state.[2] However, most accreditation bodies are regional or national. Regional

---

[1]http://www.apa.org/support/education/accreditation/importance.aspx#answer
[2]For example, here is the accrediting body for Virginia postsecondary schools: http://www.schev.edu/students/publications/POPEbrochure.pdf

accreditation refers to a set of standards set forth for schools in a group of states. There are six regional accrediting bodies:

1. Middle State Association of Colleges and Schools (Commission on Higher Education)
2. New England Association of Schools and Colleges (Commission on Technical and Career Institutions and Commission on Institutions of Higher Education)
3. North Central Association of Colleges and Schools (The Higher Learning Commission)
4. Northwest Association of Schools and Colleges
5. Southern Association of Colleges and Schools (Commission on Colleges)
6. Western Association of Schools and Colleges (Accrediting Commission for Community and Junior Colleges and Accrediting Commission for Senior Colleges and Universities).

These bodies are recognized by the Council for Higher Education Accreditation and they focus on educational quality, improvement, and accountability. Holding a regional accreditation from one of these bodies is an indicator that the school has met their minimum standards. These are the same bodies that accredit all traditional schools, including Ivy League colleges and Big 10 schools. Accreditation from one of these bodies means that the online school you are considering has met the same rigorous standards.

You can review the list of institutions that are accredited by these regional bodies online here: http://www.chea.org/Directories/regional. asp or via the Department of Education's web site here: http://ope.ed. gov/accreditation/Search.aspx.

There are also national accrediting bodies that perform quality reviews of schools based upon their program of study. For example, you can review the National Accrediting Commission of Career Arts and Sciences to assess whether your arts and sciences program is nationally accredited.[3] This will offer you a national rather than a regional comparison of schools and it is principally based upon program of study rather than overall educational approach. Again, this process is voluntary for schools.

[3]http://naccas.org/Pages/AboutNACCAS.aspx

1.7.3 Why Does Accreditation Matter?

Your ability to secure a job upon graduation often depends on having earned a degree or certificate from an accredited university. Unless your goal is to learn a skill set that you will apply in self-employment, graduation from a regionally or nationally accredited school is essential. Many employers will not recognize a graduate degree from a university that has not been accredited by a regional or national body because it has not met nationally or regionally recognized standards. Accordingly, we recommend including a review of accreditation as part of your search criteria for an online school.

1.8 CONCLUSION

Given the broad variety of schools and programs available, it is difficult *not* to find one that is appealing to you. For almost every job imaginable, you will find a school ready to train you for it. But remember that you are making a significant investment of time and money into your education. If you expect to get a solid return on your investment, you must take the time to select a school and program wisely. Don't rely only on what the school you are considering tells you. They have a vested interest in your enrollment in their program. Rather, research potential employers to find out what you will need to prepare you for your next position and a successful career track in your chosen field. Narrow your school choices down by: (1) accreditation; (2) the courses offered by the school that are relevant to your goals; (3) schedule and flexibility of the program; and (4) cost. (Note that we placed cost last not because it is less important, but rather because the first three considerations could affect the value of your degree and thus the value of your investment).

Once you have selected a school and a program and have successfully enrolled, keep an eye on the elements discussed in this chapter. If the school loses accreditation; if job placement rates drop precipitously; or if you find out that any of the data you relied upon about the school was incorrect, it is not too late to change schools. Unlike traditional universities, a change between online schools is relatively painless and does not require you to relocate. You may lose some tuition in doing so, but consider the long-term costs if your ability to find employment after graduation is significantly reduced.

1.9 CONCLUDING THOUGHTS

Take the time to make the right choice. There are many excellent schools out there that offer online programs. Finding the right one is challenging and time-consuming but well worth the effort that you dedicate. Begin your research now to prepare yourself for the long journey ahead.

CHAPTER 2

What to Expect in an Online Class and How to Prepare

Millie starts her first class online and is overwhelmed with what she sees. She does not know where to find out what assignments to complete and is not sure how to contact her professor. After a few days, she is able to contact her academic advisor and get instructions on how to navigate her way through the classroom. However, by the time she figures this out, most of her classmates have posted to the discussion board and she realizes that she has already fallen behind.

2.1 INTRODUCTION

Starting a new school is overwhelming for everyone. Starting a new school and taking your first classes online may seem daunting. However, with just a little preparation, you can ensure that you start off on the right foot and maximize your chances for success.

2.2 NAVIGATING THE CLASSROOM

Although many aspects of classes will vary from school to school, there are some ways in which nearly all classes are similar. Most schools offer a "tour" of what a typical class looks like on their web site or through an academic advisor. You can take a tour either before you decide to enroll in a school or before you begin your first class. It is a good idea to familiarize yourself with how classes are organized at your school so that you can easily navigate through your classes once they begin. If you are having a hard time finding these resources, you should ask your admissions counselor or academic advisor where to find them before you begin your first class. If you do so, once class begins, you will be ready to dive into the course material rather than worrying about where to find your first reading assignment. You will be positioned to be more successful if you are comfortable navigating the classroom before class begins so that you can focus on learning.

2.3 ORGANIZATION

Most classes are organized into "weeks" or "units." These units are typically 7 days long, although they may not run from Monday through Saturday but may follow a different academic week. For example, an academic week may run from Tuesday through Monday to give students a day after the weekend to respond to classmates on the discussion board. A week or unit in a class will typically cover a topic or set of learning objectives. Your professor is likely to group class material and assignments by week. For example, your professor may specify that in Week 1 you should read "Jones, Chapters 1–5 and participate on Discussion Board #1." Also, your professor may state that your initial post is due on the first day of the class "week." For this reason, it is important that you know how your school defines a "week" or "unit" before class begins so that you begin to participate on the very first day.

2.4 SYLLABUS

Nearly all courses will contain a syllabus or course guide. Unlike traditional schools, this may not be a single document but may be a set of links to each unit with readings and assignments listed therein. As soon as you are able to access the syllabus, you should do so. This is where you will find all information relevant to the work you will be expected to complete throughout class including reading assignments, discussion board requirements, and written assignment due dates. Once you have this information, you can begin planning your time and inserting information into your calendar. The syllabus will also list the textbooks that are required for class. You should check to ensure that you have all required course materials before class begins. If you have any questions about anything in the syllabus, you should ask your professor immediately so that you will not be scrambling to get clarification about assignments or course requirements later in the term.

2.5 MEET YOUR PROFESSOR

Most courses will have an area where you can learn more about your professor. This may be a dedicated "Meet Your Professor" area or it may be a link to the biography of your instructor. You should read this information to learn all that you can about who will be teaching—and grading—your work throughout the term. You should also take note of whether your professor might be a good source of information about careers in your field or might be a good person to ask for a reference as you approach graduation, provided you do well in his or her class.

2.6 CLASS INTRODUCTIONS

Many classes have a discussion board for students to use to introduce themselves and learn more about their classmates. Often it is required to post an introduction and respond to several classmates. Even if you are not required to respond to your classmates' introductions, it is a good practice to take the opportunity to get to know those students with whom you will be sharing a class with over the next several weeks and reach out to at least of few other students. At the very least, you should read everyone's introduction and take note of potential study group partners, those who might provide job leads, and anyone who lives in your area that you can reach out to for support. You may also find someone who has interests similar to yours and make a new friend!

2.7 OPEN DISCUSSION AREA

Most classes have some type of open discussion area where you can post questions or comments for your classmates to see. Because posts to the weekly discussion boards should be limited to the question posed by the professor for discussion, the open discussion area is where you can discuss anything not directly related to a specific assignment. The name of this area varies but may be called something like "Cyber Café" or "Let's Chat." Most professors will not check this area regularly, so you should not ask your professor questions here. But you can use it to ask your classmates for ideas for a final paper, share interesting web sites related to class, exchange recipes, organize study groups, or even announce a new job or the birth of a child. Although participation is optional, many students have found study partners, received support, and even made friends this way.

2.8 QUESTIONS FOR THE PROFESSOR

If you have a question, chances are one of your classmates has the same one. For this reason, many classes contain a discussion board where students can post general questions for their professor about class. The name of this area varies but may be called something like "Virtual Office" or "Ask the Professor." This is where you should ask your professor questions from which you think the entire class might benefit. Examples are questions about required page length for a paper, a request for clarity about a discussion board question, or more information about the late policy. As this area is visible to the entire class, you should not ask questions that relate to only you or that contain personal information. For example, you should not use this forum to ask your professor why you received a poor grade on a quiz or ask for an extension on an assignment. If you need to discuss these matters, you should contact your professor privately via e-mail or course messaging.

2.9 DISCUSSION BOARDS

With few exceptions, nearly all online classes contain weekly discussion boards or discussion forums. Discussion boards are the "heart" of many online classes. Most classes contain one or two questions for discussion each week. Students are normally required to post an in-depth response to the question asked and respond to two or more classmates each week in a substantive manner. Some classes include a minimum word requirement and may require you to include reference material to support your assertions. In most classes, the majority of your interaction with your professor and classmates will occur on the discussion boards. In nearly all online programs, these discussions take place asynchronously, which means that students post when they are able to within the unit. Posting after the unit ends is not usually accepted. This is because once a discussion ends, the focus of the course moves on to the next discussion, leaving little to no opportunity for meaningful interaction with the class. If you believe you will not be able to post during the open period for the unit, check your professor's late policy and, if necessary, contact your professor. Many schools also have requirements that students post their initial response by a set day, such as Thursday, or post on at least 2 or 3 different days of the week. These policies help ensure that there is a lively and vibrant discussion throughout the week rather than a rash of posting during the last day or two of the discussion. Check for these policies in the course materials before sending your professor a barrage of messages. The policies are usually clearly stated either in the syllabus, course announcements, or course overview.

2.10 CLASS POLICIES

In each class you take, the professor will follow policies regarding late work, penalties for plagiarism, discussion board participation, how he or she would like to be contacted, and other important class elements. Some schools have standardized policies, and some schools allow individual professors to develop their own policies. Some policies are listed and in the syllabus, and some may be listed in their own area of the class. Regardless of where the policies are found, you should be sure to read them at the beginning of class and ask your professor any questions right away.

Although many schools have policies that all professors must follow in some areas, such as for plagiarism, most schools give professors some discretion to modify policies for their classes as they see fit. This can get confusing so it is extremely important that you review the policies for each and every course that you take. Just because your last professor accepted written assignments up to a week late does not mean that your new professor will. You do not want to find this out by discovering you were awarded no points on your course project that you handed in two hours late. Similarly, if your professor has a late policy that clearly states no discussion board posts are accepted late unless you have made prior arrangements, sending him or her an e-mail asking why your late posts haven't been graded will likely get you a response referring you back to the late policy. If you had read the late policy at the beginning of the class, you would have known that you only needed to send your professor an e-mail ahead of time asking for an extension to have your work accepted.

2.11 LECTURES

Some, but not all, courses contain lectures. These may be recorded, asynchronous lectures that you can listen to at your own convenience anytime during the week, or they may be live, synchronous lectures that you must attend at a certain time. As most online courses are designed for students who need flexibility, if your course contains synchronous lectures, it is very likely that a recorded archive of the lecture will be available for students who are unable to attend. However, be sure you understand the policies related to synchronous lectures before missing one so that you do not unnecessarily lose points.

For example, you may be required to listen to an archived live lecture before the end of the week or you may be required to draft a summary of the lecture in order to be eligible for points. It is very important that you attend or listen to all lecture material provided. During lectures, your professor may highlight information that he or she feels is important in your reading material—this will offer important insights into what your professor will be looking for when grading your work. Your professor may also provide you with information and knowledge not found in your reading and may offer tips and suggestions for completing assignments.

2.12 ANNOUNCEMENTS

In any course that you take online, your professor will likely post announcements to communicate important information related to the course with the entire class. Announcements are generally visible when you log into your course and you should regularly check for new announcements that your professor has posted. Some professors post weekly announcements introducing students to the material that will be covered that week and some may post guidance regarding assignments. Some professors may provide links to additional resources or videos as announcements and some may share internship or grant opportunities. Regardless of how your professor uses announcements, you will be responsible for any information your professor has posted as an announcement. Be sure to read each announcement and contact your professor if you have questions.

2.13 E-MAIL OR MESSAGES

Even though you will not see your professor in person, most professors who teach classes online are readily available to students via e-mail or messaging depending on the type of system used by the school. Most professors will list their e-mail address in the syllabus or in a course announcement. Before you send a question to your professor, be certain that you have thoroughly reviewed the course materials to ensure that the answer is not readily available. When a professor receives an e-mail asking a question that is easily answered via materials that are already posted, the professor may begin to question the diligence with which you prepare your assignments.

When you e-mail or send a message to your professor, be sure your e-mail is courteous, professional, and specific. Compare the two e-mails below:

Hey Prof,

What's up with this assignment? I'm confussed. Help!

Mikey

~ ~

Dear Professor Milton,

I am in your Introduction to Political Science class, POL 101, Section 02, C Term. For the week two assignment, we are to discuss the texting and driving laws that apply to us. However, I am not sure if you would like us to discuss state or city laws or both. Please let me know.

Thank you for your time.

Sincerely,

Michael Jacobs

The first e-mail does not contain enough information to allow the professor to respond to the student quickly because it does not contain the class name or number, let the professor know with which assignment the student is having trouble or with which part of the assignment the student is struggling. The e-mail does not even contain the student's full name. Moreover, the student's e-mail contains a spelling error. The professor is not likely to be left with a favorable impression of this student after reading this e-mail.

Now consider the second e-mail. This e-mail opens with a proper greeting (Dear so-and-so) and uses the professor's title (Professor) and name. This is a polite way to address your professor and sets a good tone for the rest of the e-mail. The student then tells the professor exactly which class he or she is in (course name, number, section, and term) to enable the professor to locate the right class quickly. The student then goes on to identify the specific assignment, when the assignment is due (in which week), and also tells the professor the topic. The student then lets professor know *exactly* which part of the assignment is giving him trouble. Before closing the e-mail, the student thanks the professor for his or her time. Finally, the student ends with a respectful closing (Sincerely) and gives the professor his full name. The professor is left with the impression that this student is serious, careful, and cares about his grade.

2.14 ASSIGNMENTS

Nearly every course requires at least one or two written assignments in addition to discussion board postings and, in some cases, quizzes, or exams. These assignments usually take the form of papers that examine a topic in-depth. The assignment due dates, or week in which the assignment is due, will be listed in the syllabus. The syllabus may provide more specific information about the assignments, such as the topic and page length requirement, or may simply note that a written assignment is due in a particular week. Additional information about written assignments can be found in the course homepage. Some schools provide a single link within the course homepage to all assignments, and other schools will provide links to assignments under the weeks in which they are due. Regardless of how your school organizes classes, links to assignments should be clearly labeled. Early in the term, make sure you take note of any assignments that are due early in the term, understand their requirements, and allot sufficient time to complete your work.

2.15 TESTS AND QUIZZES

If your class requires that you take tests or quizzes, they will be listed in the syllabus. You will see links to these within the course homepage. As with assignments, some schools have a single link you will use to access all tests and quizzes in the course and others provide links to tests and quizzes under the week in which you are required to take them. Wherever the link is located, your tests and quizzes will be clearly labeled. As with assignments, early in the term make sure that you take note of any tests or quizzes required and allot enough time to study for the exams and take them. In some cases, you will be permitted to retake a quiz after speaking with your professor and explaining why you missed it or performed poorly on it. Check your professor's policy on retaking quizzes at the start of the class.

2.16 ADDITIONAL OR SUPPLEMENTAL MATERIAL

Some professors will want you to read material that it is not included in your class textbooks. This material may be mandatory or optional. If your professor would like you to review additional or supplemental material, it should be listed in the syllabus. When you begin a class, you should specifically look for supplemental material to help ensure that you do not miss any references to any information that will help you understand the course material and do better in class. How this information is provided varies greatly. Some professors may provide videos, some may provide written notes, some may provide links to Internet sources, and some may provide links to scholarly journals in the school library. Even if the additional material is optional, you should plan on reviewing it to ensure you learn as much as you can and can offer as much insight into the topic as possible in your discussion posts and papers.

2.17 CONCLUDING THOUGHTS

Now that you know what to expect from the typical online class and what you can do to prepare, you should feel more confident starting a new school online. Taking the time to familiarize yourself with your learning environment, your professor's expectations, and any other resources available to you will greatly reduce your stress level, save you time, and position you for success.

CHAPTER 3

What You Will Miss and How to Make Up for it

Mary loves to debate. She has no problem playing devil's advocate and engaging in spirited discussion. Mary is concerned that she will miss out on such interactions with classmates and her professor if she attends school online.

Dave is thinking about going to school online. However, he is in his late 30s and has been out of school for a while. He thinks he will have a lot of questions for his professors but doesn't know how he will ask them if he never sees his professors in person.

3.1 INTRODUCTION

When deciding whether an online school is right for you, may wonder what you will miss by not attending a traditional brick-and-mortar school. When you attend school online, you will not see your classmates on a regular basis, have a face-to-face conversation with your professor, or go to the Student Union for a club meeting. While it is true that online schools will never be able to offer some things that are found on most college campuses, you may be surprised the differences between the two are not extreme. Moreover, there are some steps you can take as an online student to ensure that you receive many of the same experiences and benefits of traditional schools.

3.2 ACCESS TO PROFESSORS

On a traditional college campus, students attend live classes, can stay after class to ask their professor questions, and have the option of meeting with their professor during their professor's office hours. You may wonder whether a professor teaching an online class will be as accessible—the answer is a resounding yes. Most online schools provide numerous ways of contacting your professor.

Many schools have an area in the classroom dedicated solely to asking your professor questions. This area serves as a "virtual office" and can be used to ask your professor anything that is of general interest to the class since it is visible to all students. This is an ideal place to go to ask your professor questions about course requirements, assignments, or to clarify a discussion question. As you will be entering your classroom several times a week, this is a very accessible area of the classroom.

Nearly all professors will provide you with their e-mail address or another way to send them a message. Most professors check for messages from students at least once a day and will respond to you very quickly, usually within 24 hours. You should never hesitate to e-mail your professor if you have a question about your grade, are struggling with an assignment, or to ask for career advice.

Some professors also give their phone numbers to students. If your professor gives you his or her phone number, you should call with any concerns you have about class that may not be easily addressed over e-mail. If you do call, be sure to call only during the hours your professor has said he or she will available to speak or, better yet, make an appointment. Even if your professor does not provide a phone number at the beginning of class, if you would like to talk to your professor on the phone, you should send your professor your phone number and ask him or her to call—most will! Just be sure to include a short note about what you would like to discuss so that your professor can be prepared for the conversation.

Different schools offer other means of contacting professors, including making instant messaging available, being able to "chat" with your professor online, and requiring professors to hold "live" office hours using the school's platform.

No matter which online school you choose to attend, you can rest assured that your professor will be available to answer your questions, give you advice, and help you through difficult assignments.

3.3 LECTURES

Most traditional schools require students to attend live lectures one or more times each week. Professors usually provide a lot of information during lectures, and you may be concerned about whether you will learn as much in an online class as those able to attend lectures on campuses. Online schools usually strive to provide an education equal, or better, to educations received on traditional campuses. Most schools provide the same information presented in traditional lectures, although the approach may vary.

Some online schools hold live online lectures to try to replicate the traditional lecture held in a traditional school where students and the professor are in the same place at the same time. This is a wonderful opportunity for you to interact with your classmates and instructor if your school offers this option and you are able to log on at the time the lecture is held. However, bear in mind that in order to offer their students maximum flexibility in completing their coursework, most online schools do not offer live lectures. The typical online student is extremely busy juggling multiple responsibilities and cannot commit to attending a weekly live session.

Several schools offer weekly recorded lectures that can be accessed at any time during the week. This gives you the same experience as listening to an expert on the topic, but because these lectures are available at your convenience, you can listen to the lecture in small portions if you find you absorb the material better that way or if that approach works better for your schedule. Many students find this approach suits them better than sitting through a long lecture on which they find they cannot concentrate. Another benefit of being able to access a lecture at your convenience is that you can review the lecture multiple times if you are struggling with the material.

Other schools choose to present material in an entirely different manner. These schools will provide additional course material, usually in the form of written lessons that contain the type of information usually found in traditional lectures. These lessons are also available at any time and are easy to review. Some students prefer having all material presented in a written format since they can review the material wherever they are and whenever they like.

As you can see, far from missing out essential material, online schools have various ways of presenting the same information given in traditional live lectures. By attending school online, you will able to learn all of the same material without spending time in a large, anonymous lecture hall at a time scheduled for the convenience of the professor.

3.4 CLASS DISCUSSION

In traditional schools, professors may begin class with a scenario for the class to consider. There is often a lively and interesting discussion in the classroom. Students debate and emerge with better analytical skills and greater knowledge.

Nearly all online schools have similar discussions in the classroom. Most online classrooms contain weekly discussion boards in which professors present students with a question to answer and discuss throughout the week. In order to be certain there is interaction between students, most professors will require students to not just post an original response to the question but to also respond to at least one or two classmates. The professor will follow the discussion closely throughout the week. Depending on the direction the discussion takes, the professor will post additional information, ask additional questions, and make connections between various student posts. Don't be surprised if the professor does not respond directly to you each week—this is not because you did a bad job in your posting. More than likely, it is because you were on point and the professor wanted to focus on shaping the discussion through postings that veered off topic instead.

These discussions can be as lively as any that take place in a traditional classroom. Holding discussions virtually, over an extended period of time, can also allow you to get more out of class because you can take the time to form thoughtful responses rather than just saying whatever comes to you while sitting in an hour-long class. This format also allows your professor the flexibility to tailor the discussion to the interests of your particular class rather than sticking to the notes he or she brought to class.

3.5 LIBRARY

Most traditional schools have large libraries full of books, journals, and magazines. Students at these schools can use the library to find all the resources necessary for their assignments. You may be concerned that you will not have access to the same resources if you attend school online. While you will not likely have the experience of sifting through volumes on the shelves, you will have access to most of the same information.

Most online schools have vast online libraries that contain not just books, but scholarly journals and newspaper and magazine articles. Although your online school may not have all the same reference books available as a traditional university, nearly all of the same information will be available in electronic form through alternate or secondary sources. Your school will likely have a library staff that can help orient you to the resources available and how to access them. University librarians can also help you with any research questions you may have while writing papers for any class throughout your schooling.

Additionally, do not overlook resources that may be available to you locally. If you are more comfortable performing research with books you can touch, you should also explore your local public library. Librarians at your public library will also be able to help you to perform research and answer questions you may have about the variety of sources available to you. Most public libraries also have computers available for public use which may allow you to keep current with your coursework if your computer breaks.

If you live near a traditional university, you may be able to access their library for free or a small annual fee. The rules regarding access to university libraries vary widely, but if there is such a library convenient to you, it is worth exploring whether you will be able to utilize their resources.

3.6 STUDY GROUPS

Students at traditional schools sit in classrooms with their peers and have the opportunity to speak with each other before and after class. In doing so, they may form study groups to help them review and organize course material.

You may feel that you may not be able to form study groups while taking online classes. However, many students taking online classes have been able to form study groups that have helped them succeed. Your study group can coordinate via telephone or e-mail—there need not be in-person meetings to work together to review material, create study guides, and get input on ideas for discussion board posts or papers. Virtual study groups can be just as effective as those formed on traditional campuses, if not more so, as everyone can work at the time that works best for them. If you are interested in finding out more about how to form a study group and how you can benefit from one, you can find out more in Chapter 4 on study habits.

3.7 FRIENDS

One rewarding part of attending a university is making new friends who share your interests. Many friendships formed on college campuses last a lifetime. You may be concerned that by attending school online, you will miss out on the opportunity to meet new people and form such rewarding relationships. However, online schools offer ways in which you can meet your classmates and form new friendships.

Most of your classes will have a discussion board where students introduce themselves. You should post your introduction there and let your classmates know that you are interested in forming relationships outside of class. You should also read each of your classmates' introductions. You will likely find at least a couple of students in each class who share your interests and a few others who are facing the same challenges as you, whether it is attending school while raising a family, traveling frequently, having been recently laid off, or making a change to the same field as you. You can reach out to these students to let them know more about yourself. You may find that you are soon e-mailing regularly, sharing your phone number, and even registering for future classes together.

Some schools offer an instant messaging or chat feature to their students. If your school offers this option, you may want to log in frequently and see who else is online. You can casually chat with classmates you see online to see if you have anything in common or just talk about how class is going. You may find yourself chatting with your classmates for quite some time and wanting to continue your conversation.

A very simple way to form new friendships with your classmates is to let others in your class know that you are open to making new friends. Some students will post their personal e-mail addresses in the student café or in their introduction and let their classmates know that they would like to hear from them. Additionally, most students tell their classmates where they live in their introduction. If you do so as well, you can ask if anyone lives in your area and would like to meet for coffee or lunch. You may be surprised to learn that you have a classmate living close by that you can meet in person.

3.8 STUDENT ORGANIZATIONS

Many traditional universities offer students ways to further explore their academic and professional interests by joining student organizations or clubs. These organizations can help you make connections within your field and connect you to other students who share your interests.

Traditional universities are not the only place such organizations and clubs are found. Most online schools have student organizations that meet virtually. A list of a school's organizations can usually be found on its web site. Student organizations at online schools range from psychology clubs, to anime student groups, to honor societies. You can make valuable contacts and meet likeminded people by joining a club if you have time.

3.9 CONCLUDING THOUGHTS

Even though online schools differ from traditional universities in many respects, it is very easy to gain the same access to information, resources, and professors. In most cases, it is easier as you access what and whom you need on your own schedule from wherever is most convenient for you.

Strategies for Success in Online Education

Forming Good Habits to Reduce Stress, Find a Work–Life Balance, and Succeed in School

Max feels like he is always on the run. He wishes he had more time to study, but he feels like every minute of his day is already scheduled and doesn't know how he can fit in additional studying.

4.1 INTRODUCTION

It is easy to get overwhelmed with how much you need to accomplish if you do not have a clear plan to get it all done. It is also easy to start feeling resentful toward work and school obligations if you think you are missing out on other parts of life, such as time with friends and family. Forming good habits to get, and stay, organized early on in your academic career will help make your time in school less stressful, more enjoyable, and most importantly, make you more successful.

4.2 GETTING ORGANIZED

4.2.1 Use a Calendar

Most online students deal with multiple demands on their time. It is essential to find a system that helps you stay organized and on-track. Your final grade will suffer if you fall behind in your required reading or miss deadlines for class assignments. Having a system in place at the beginning of class to ensure this does not happen will give you an advantage over your classmates and put you on the path to success.

To be organized it is essential to use a calendar. You should use one calendar to keep track of school, work, family, and social obligations to ensure you are able to fit in everything that needs to get done and make adjustments to your schedule when it's needed. That may sound easy enough, but in order to be certain you create a system that works, you should give some thought to what kind of calendar works best. If you usually use the calendar on your computer or phone to schedule a work and social event, you should follow that same method to keep track of your schoolwork. If you usually use a paper calendar to keep track of your schedule, stay with that approach. Another consideration is the view you should use. Whether you use an electronic or physical calendar, consider how far in advance you like to plan. If you normally create plans far in advance, you should use a calendar with a month view. If you can only plan a week at a time, a calendar with a weekly view is best for you.

Once you have your calendar, you should identify the different categories you will be writing on your calendar and assigning each one a color. For example, work obligations could be written in blue, time with family in purple, social events in red, and schoolwork in orange. Using different colors will let you know at a glance what your day, week, or month holds in store. As you develop the habit of associating a color with a type of event, you will be able to more effectively manage your increasingly crowded schedule.

You should start your calendaring process by writing down obligations you cannot change. Write down your work hours as soon as you know them. If you will be caring for children every day from the time you pick them up from school until the time they go to bed, write that down as well. Even if your schedule includes events that are always going to occur on certain days or times, having a visual reminder of your other obligations will help you identify the best time to study.

Once you have done this, you are ready to fill in school obligations. This will be a two-step process that involves first writing down due dates and then setting aside time to complete your assignments and review of course material.

As soon as you get your class syllabus, write down when all assignments are due in the color you have chosen to record schoolwork. If discussion board posts are due on Thursdays, be sure to write that information down on each Thursday for the duration of the term. Also fill in any deadlines for tests and papers. Many students also find it helpful to include reminders or "ticklers" for assignments. This means that if your discussion board post is due on Thursday, you may want to put on your calendar that you should start working on your post on Tuesday. If you use Google or Outlook as your calendar, you should be able to add a reminder to the event so that you get a "ding" when your postings or assignments are nearly due. If you are required to take a quiz each Sunday, you should note on your calendar that you will need time to study for the quiz earlier the week. For larger assignments, such as final papers due the last week of class, you should create a schedule for yourself that you will follow throughout the term. For example, if your paper is due in week 11 of a class, you should note on your calendar that you should have your topic chosen by week two, research complete by week four, an outline by week five, a draft by week eight, a draft submitted to the school's writing center by week nine, and a final revision complete by week 10.

In addition to completing assignments, you will also be required to examine course materials, which may include required reading, listening to lectures, and visiting web sites. Consider these requirements with deadlines for completion and note the deadlines on your calendar. Decide at the beginning of the term when you would like to have your review of course material completed. This should be done as early in the week as possible to allow you sufficient time to work on discussion board posts and other assignments that are due that week. Once you have decided on these self-imposed deadlines, write them on your calendar. For example, you may want to have your weekly reading done by Monday each week and your review of the weekly lecture done by Tuesday.

After you have filled in due dates for all assignments and created a schedule to keep you on track, you should figure out how much time it will take to complete these assignments and schedule time to do so. You should approximate the amount of time it will take to complete all assignments and examine course material each week and block off time of in your calendar to get your work done. This will let you know if you have time to pick up another shift or if you need to turn down an invitation for drinks because you will need more time to work on a paper.

If possible, it is helpful to have a consistent schedule for studying and to set aside at least a little time for schoolwork each day. For example, you may plan to do schoolwork for one hour on Monday night, two hours on Tuesday afternoon, one hour each Wednesday, Thursday, and Friday evening, five hours on Saturday afternoon, and a half-hour to check-in to your class on Sunday. Having a consistent schedule will help you ensure that you have the time you need to get the best grades you can. If you find you have set aside too much time for schoolwork for a given class, you can always cut back. It is better to err on the side of caution when creating a schedule and ensure you have allotted all the time you think you will need. You should also be realistic about the amount of time it will take to complete assignments such as term papers or studying for final exams. Because you will have those assignments written on your calendar at the beginning of the term, you should schedule additional time for completing schoolwork in weeks in which additional work is required.

4.3 CREATING MANAGEABLE GOALS

When you begin an online degree program, your ultimate goal is to complete all required courses, graduate, and presumably get a job in your chosen field. Looking at the long list of classes you need to reach that goal may make you feel like that goal is unobtainable. However, when you look at each individual class and make the completion of each class a goal in and of itself, you will start to feel like you can accomplish anything one step at a time. However, there are steps you can take to break each class, and even each assignment, down into smaller, more manageable goals that can help you complete your work more quickly and with less stress.

When you start each new class, you will likely receive a syllabus or course guide laying out all of the work that is required for the term. When you open the syllabus, you will likely see hundreds of pages of reading, several required discussion boards, at least a few papers, and may be an exam or two. Many students look at the long list required work and wonder how they can possibly get it all done and still work, not become a stranger to their family, and keep up with other obligations. You do not need to complete all classwork at once, and setting goals will help you stay focused and get the work done without feeling overwhelmed by everything that needs to be accomplished before the end of the term.

Weekly goals: When you see a syllabus for a new class for the first time, take a deep breath. Remind yourself that you do not need to complete all of this work at once or even in a couple of weeks. In fact, you only need to complete a small portion each week and that should be your weekly goal. Instead of looking at the syllabus as a whole document, break it down into smaller syllabi—one for each week of the term. You will likely find focusing on the relatively small amount of required work each week is a manageable goal. You may not feel as overwhelmed, and completing your weekly goals will seem like a manageable task.

Daily goals: Even after realizing that your weekly goal is manageable, you still need a strategy to achieve those goals. Moreover, looking at what you have to do in a given week, there may be times when you will still wonder how to get it all done. You can further break down each week's assignments into even smaller chunks that you want to accomplish each day. By doing this, you will see that accomplishing a small goal of getting a portion of your work done each day can easily be done. This approach also allows you to set smaller goals for yourself on days when other obligations, such as a long shift at work or your daughter's ballet recital, may leave little time for schoolwork. You can then set a larger goal for yourself on days when you will not have as many competing obligations.

Discrete goals: Your daily goals can be broken into even smaller goals in order to help you plan your day. Instead of looking at all of the reading you have to do for the week as one assignment, you can break down your reading assignments even further. For example, look at the 10 pages of reading you have to get done from Text A as one goal to accomplish and the 20 pages of reading you have to complete from Text B as a second goal. You may find that setting discrete goals will reduce stress related to completing schoolwork and allow you to fit more activities into your life. You may not be able to read all 30 pages on your bus ride to work, but if you set reading 10 pages from Text A as its own goal, you just may find you can accomplish one of your daily goals during time that would otherwise have been wasted.

Remember to record your weekly and daily goals on your calendar. Checking off the goals you have accomplished at the end of each day will give you a great sense of satisfaction and clearly show you how much progress you are making toward reaching your ultimate goal of holding your diploma in your hand. A great trick to stay motivated in achieving goals is to write them down on an index card or small square of paper and tape them to the refrigerator or somewhere you will see them every day. You can't avoid them if they are always in front of you!

4.4 MANAGING YOUR INBOX CLUTTER

Everyone's inbox can fill up quickly with e-mails from friends, work, merchants, and a variety of other sources. While you are in school, your inbox will also fill up with e-mail from the university, your professors, your classmates, and eventually potential employers. It is important you develop a system for keeping track of your e-mails so that you do not miss anything important that could make a difference or your grade, registering for the classes you want, or making the key connection that could give you the edge in getting the job you want after graduation.

Many students find it convenient to have one e-mail account where all of their e-mail goes to reduce time spent checking multiple e-mail accounts. If you prefer this method, you may be able to set up your school's e-mail account to be automatically forwarded to your central account. Some students prefer to keep school e-mails separate from their other e-mails and choose to use their school e-mail account exclusively for correspondence related to school—either approach is fine.

Regardless of whether you choose to use one e-mail account or two while in school, you should develop and use a foldering or labeling system for your incoming mail. At a minimum, you should have separate folders for each class, administrative matters, potential contacts, and personal issues.

A list of folders related to school might look like this:

- Political Science 100
- American Government 201
- Financial Aid
- Tech Support
- Job Leads
- Networking Connections
- Friends.

If you choose to use a central e-mail account for all e-mail, you should create additional folders related to specific work projects, events, online orders, and any other area in which you frequently send or receive e-mails.

This system is simple to implement and will help you stay organized and find the information you need quickly. Keep in mind that not every e-mail is created equally. If you do not feel the need to label an e-mail in your inbox, you should immediately delete it to reduce inbox clutter. For example, if your school sends you an e-mail advertising new sweatshirts with the school logo and you have no interest in buying one, do not hesitate to delete it right away and not give it another thought.

4.5 CREATING A STUDY KIT

Even if you are taking classes online, there will still be some things other than your computer that you will need to use regularly. You may be required to use textbooks and you may choose to use old-fashioned pen and paper or notecards to take notes. You should create a "study kit" to help you save time by having everything you need in one place. Creating a study kit is easy and will save you time in the long run. Simply choose a bag or box and fill it with everything you need to study. If you do this, you will never find yourself wasting valuable study time looking for your lost textbook or the colored pens you use to keep track of assignments. Your study kit should also include anything you use to reward yourself for getting your work done, whether it be a chocolate bar or a $5 gift card for iTunes. A study kit will also ensure that you have everything that you need if you travel or need to study somewhere other than home, such as a café or library.

4.6 PREPARING FOR THE WORST-CASE SCENARIO

At some point while you are in school, you will find yourself dealing with an unexpected situation. It could be finding yourself without power, dealing with a sick babysitter, or having your work schedule changed unexpectedly. When such situations occur, they cause additional stress, in large part because you have to scramble to find a solution while still getting your work done. You can reduce the stress that comes along with dealing with worst-cases scenario situations by preparing for them in advance. Before school starts, you should anticipate the types of occurrences that have the potential to throw you off-track and have a plan in place so that you can keep up with school no matter what. Below are some common worst-case scenario situations and the steps you can take to prevent them from becoming catastrophes.

1. *Losing Internet access*: No matter who or where you are, you may lose Internet access at any moment if your Internet provider experiences problems. Depending on where you live, you also may experience storms with the potential to unexpectedly knock out power and your Internet connection. If this happens, know where you can

access the Internet if you lose power. Our students have been able to use the Internet connections at coffee shops, libraries, friend's houses, and even hotel lobbies when they found themselves without power. Before you begin school, do a little bit of research to find out where you will able to access the Internet in the event you lose your connection. Keep in mind that, after power outages, commercial areas usually have their power restored before residential areas, so it is worth checking to see if your local mall or shopping center has any cafes, restaurants, or stores that provide Internet access.

2. *Not enough childcare*: No matter how well you plan, at some point in your schooling, you will find yourself without a babysitter when you need one either because your childcare provider is sick or your schoolwork is taking up more time than you anticipated. This need not be a reason to panic if you are prepared. Before school begins, make a list of friends, family, and potential babysitters, and ask them if they will be able to help you with childcare if needed in a pinch. At the beginning of each term, touch base with everyone on your list and ask them if they are still able to help. You should keep the list up-to-date with new people who might be available to help. When you find yourself needing an extra two hours to write your final paper for a class, instead of wracking your brain for someone who can watch your kids, you can simply go to your list and make one or two calls to free up the time you need to do your best in school. This is most likely to occur in the last week or two of the term when you may have a final exam or final paper due. Being prepared will reduce stress since you know you will be able to get your work done no matter what.

3. *Unexpected changes in your work schedule*: No matter how well you plan, you are bound to be asked to change your shift at work, put in extra hours, or travel for work. You may not feel as though as you can say no to such requests. You need not worry about such last-minute changes to your schedule if you have thought about what to do in advance. Because you should have all obligations for work and school and to family and friends written on the same calendar, the first thing you should do is see if there is something you can change to make some additional time for schoolwork. If your calendar is well organized, you should be able to identify such events at a glance. You may be disappointed to have to cancel dinner with your significant other or a movie with your best friend, but those people who really care about you will understand because

they want you to succeed. If there is truly nothing on your calendar you can change, you can approach the lost time in small increments. If you cannot find a two hour chunk of time in your schedule, identify somewhere that you can add 15 or 20 minutes of study time. This may mean adding a little time onto the time you have already set aside to study or fitting in a little reading over your lunch break.

4.7 ALWAYS REVIEW FEEDBACK

Most professors teaching online classes will provide you with an abundance of feedback beginning the first week of class and continuing throughout the term. In order to position yourself to do well in class, you should review all feedback your professor gives you on every assignment, no matter how you feel you are doing in class. All of your professors want to see you succeed, and most will tell you exactly how you can improve your grade or what you should continue to do to keep the A you already have. There are many reasons to review your professor's feedback.

1. *No news is not always good news*: You may think you are meeting your professor's expectations on the discussion board because your professor does not follow up on your posts with a suggestion for improvement or because he or she does not comment at all. You should not assume that "no news is good news" when it comes to discussion board posts. Many professors are reluctant to point out errors in discussion boards and other public areas of the classroom that are accessible to all students and so will rarely respond to discussion board posts with suggestions about how you can improve your post or criticism of any kind. However, most professors will leave feedback for you privately, letting you know exactly what you need to do to improve your grade. Conversely, good news is usually good news. You should review all feedback your professor leaves on the discussion board regardless of whether it is directed toward you. If your professor comments that any post is good, well-written, or insightful, he or she is letting all students know what he or she considers to be A-level work. Pay attention and your grade will go up.

2. *Your grade does not say it all*: If you are doing well in class and pleased with your grade, you may think that you know what you are doing and do not need to read your professor's feedback.

However, even if you are doing well in class, reviewing your professor's feedback will let you know what he or she thinks you are doing right so you know what continue to do to meet, or exceed, his or her expectations. Moreover, some professors will give students a "warning" the first time they see a mistake without deducting any points but will deduct points if they see the same error a second or third time. If your grade is anything less than perfect, you should incorporate any suggestions your professor makes. You may see your grade jump from an A- to A by doing so. This not only improves your grade in class but will improve your overall GPA.

3. *Not all professors are created alike*: If you have taken classes online before and earned high grades, you may assume that you know what is expected and think that you do not need to review what new professors are saying about your work. This is a trap you should avoid. Although some online schools may have similar policies or grading rubrics in every class, professors have the discretion to use their judgment when grading. Every professor will have their own view of what constitutes A-quality work and may interpret even standardized policies differently. The only way to know what your professor is looking for is to read the feedback he or she leaves for you.

4.8 AVOIDING BURNOUT

Even the most ambitious and energetic students are susceptible to burnout. When you reach this stage, you may lose motivation to enjoy even the tasks related to school that you most enjoy. Once you regain your momentum, you may discover that you are too far behind to catch-up. There are simple steps you can take to help yourself stay motivated and focused.

4.9 REWARD YOURSELF

There is no doubt about it—succeeding in an online program is a lot of work. Your hard work will pay off, but if you are at the beginning of your program, it may seem like the dream job with the higher salary is far off. You should not need to wait years, or even months, to reward yourself for your hard work. Rewards can be big or small. You can give them to yourself at scheduled intervals, such as a dinner out at your favorite restaurant at the end of each term. Or, you can reward yourself each time you complete one of your discrete goals, such as by allowing yourself a bite-sized chocolate bar each time you complete a reading assignment. Knowing you have something to look forward to if you are successful will help motivate you to get your work done and do it well.

4.10 SCHEDULE DOWNTIME

One very simple way to avoid burnout is to schedule breaks. While scheduling time to relax may seem like an odd idea, making sure you take some time to spend on something you enjoy will help you stay focused longer. You may find that giving yourself five minutes of downtime after every half-hour of studying, or 10 minutes after each hour, will leave you feeling refreshed and ready to hit the books (or the keyboard) with renewed energy. You should use this time to do something you enjoy, such as checking your personal e-mail or making a quick call to your best friend. Do not spend your scheduled breaks on catching up on other obligations, such as paying bills, or you will not get the benefit of relaxation and renewal that these breaks can provide.

4.11 DO NOT MULTITASK

With the vast array of devices available at our fingertips, it may seem tempting to read your textbook sitting in front of the TV or complete your discussion board posts while texting with your friend. However, trying to multitask is rarely, if ever, a good idea. You may be able to justify reading in front of the TV by telling yourself you are saving time because you will not have to watch your favorite show later. However, the reality is that because you are not giving your full attention to reading, you will likely have to reread the material at some point if you want to do well on your assignments. When your professor assigns you reading, it is because he or she wants you to absorb the material—you will not be able to do so when your attention is divided. When it comes time to demonstrate that you understand the material on a paper, discussion board post, or exam, chances are you are going to have to pull out your book again to review the material to see what you missed when you were trying to follow "Hawaii 5-0." The same is true of trying to complete a discussion board post, paper, or exam. If you are not giving your full attention to your assignment, you are more likely to write poorly and make careless mistakes. Your professor will notice and your grade will suffer.

If you are having a hard time focusing, you should take steps to remove the distractions. There are small steps you can take to make it more difficult for yourself to multitask. If you find that you are tempted to turn on the TV, the simplest solution is to never study in the same room as the TV. If that does not work, you can put the remote control in a different room or even unplug the TV when you sit down to study. If you find that you cannot stop checking for new texts when you should be researching for your term paper, you should put your phone in another room or turn it off completely. If you find that you are constantly checking Internet sites, there are steps you can take to reduce the temptation to surf the web when you should be doing schoolwork. Although you will need your computer to complete nearly all work for an online class, you will not always need the Internet. When you are working on tasks that do not require Internet access, such as reading chapters you have downloaded to your computer or writing a discussion board post, you can disable your Internet on your computer or physically unplug your Internet connection. You can also put up roadblocks to checking your favorite sites by removing them from your favorites menu or autocomplete. If you find that you cannot stop yourself from playing games installed on your computer, you can remove them from your desktop so that it takes a few more clicks to play. There are endless ways to multitask, but these strategies should give you ideas about how you can put up roadblocks to the temptation to multitask and be more productive. You can always get your phone or turn your Internet connection back on when it is time for you to give yourself a reward to take a scheduled break.

4.12 CONCLUDING THOUGHTS

If you use the strategies discussed in this chapter, you will find that you will create good habits that will reduce stress and give you more time for your friends and family. Creating good habits may be a struggle at first, but once your good habits are established, you will continue to reap the rewards for years to come.

CHAPTER 5

Managing Your Time Effectively

Robert takes the first step to realizing his lifelong goal of obtaining a college degree by enrolling in an online program. However, just a few weeks into his first class, he finds himself overwhelmed with school, work, and family obligations. He sits down and figures out ways to make small changes to his schedule that have a big impact. He finds a better balance and is able to complete his first course with an A.

5.1 INTRODUCTION

How many times have you heard the expression, "there aren't enough hours in the day," or, "I just don't have time to do it all"? Sometimes it seems that the day is too short and we will never finish what we want to in order to achieve our goals. We pass up opportunities to go to school, take a second job, read a book that can put us on the path to success (like this one), or attend a networking event, simply because there is not enough time in the day to fit in one more thing.

But why is it that our days are so busy? Is it because we suddenly have more responsibilities than we had before? Is it because our workplace is making us stay later than usual? Or is it because the day really *is* getting shorter? Well, perhaps it is all of these things. But those are not what give most people the perception that there is not enough time to accomplish everything that you would like to do. Rather, it is how we fill our free time and the fiction of nonessential obligations that we have created for ourselves that creates this perception. In other words, distractions make us feel this way.

Distractions are the enemy of the successful online student. And they are exacerbated by the type of learning environment that you find at online universities. As we discuss elsewhere in this book, one of the significant advantages of pursuing your educational dreams through an online degree program is that you have the flexibility to attend classes on your own schedule, from any location with Internet, and to proceed at your own pace. However, this also creates a serious risk of inattention to your classes and delayed performance. Consider these examples of real students (the names have been changed) we have had in our classes.

Angela is a long-haul truck driver. She always dreamed of going to college, but she is never in the same city for more than a day or two. She enrolled in an online university. Now, she completes her discussion requirements when she stops into truck rest areas and submits stellar work on time and on point. She was recommended for a student award.

Tommy is a part-time clerk at a video store. He enrolled in an online program hoping to enhance his career options and move into a better job. He enjoys the flexibility of online classes but frequently submits late and poorly done assignments because he gets distracted with his job search or watching movies. He is on academic probation and may not complete his degree.

Suzanne is a stay-at-home mother to four young children. She wants to set a good example for her children by attending college and hopes to use her degree to obtain a job that pays well with regular hours once all of her children are in school. She is unable to attend a traditional university due to her family obligations. By attending school online she is able to complete her classwork during her children's naps and after they go to sleep. She doesn't have to worry about missing class if one of her children are sick or she wants to go on a field trip. It's hard work, but Suzanne feels pride in doing what is necessary to ensure a better future for herself and her children.

Bob has a good job with the government. He excels in his position but cannot progress because he does not have a graduate degree. Bob discovered that by enrolling in an online university he can keep his job, travel as needed for work, and still keep up with class. After he obtains his degree, he expects that he will be promoted quickly to a position with more responsibility—and higher pay.

There are many types of online students from many walks of life, but each online student has demands on his or her time, and each must find the right way to integrate their educational goals into his or her life. And most importantly, each has to learn how to avoid distractions and focus on the most important goal of this entire process—learning.

In this chapter, we will endeavor to help you identify distractions in your life that are taking valuable time that could be spent on much more productive or important things. We do not intend to discount the value of doing nothing. In fact, we believe that you should take advantage of opportunities to rest and ponder the clouds from time to time as such down-time plays an important role in rejuvenation and helping to maintain focus. Instead, we will offer you a new way to structure your day that opens up chunks of time that you may have overlooked—time that you can use to advance your career through education.

This is not a traditional lecture in time management. While it is certainly important to be organized with your time and maintain a good planner, what we are doing here is actually modifying how you value time. Instead of working to maximize your existing free time, our goal here is to help you find new free time. By adopting an intuitive prioritization approach, you will find new ways to get the most out of the day.

5.2 SECTION 1: MORNINGS

Let's start from the beginning. Are you a morning person? Do you wake up rested and excited to start your day? If so, you are a lucky—and rare—person. No matter how much we enjoy getting things done in the morning, even the best of us know that it is tough to transition from a soft, warm bed to a hard, cold chair in front of a computer. So, we tend to stretch this process out as much as possible.

For many people, breakfast on a workday means a cereal bar in the car, a bagel on the road, or some other transportable condiment at the office. Some of us don't even bother with breakfast. What if I told you that not only can you enjoy a good breakfast at home and still get to the office on time, but that you can also help yourself stay in shape at the same time? This will take a few minor adjustments, but the changes are small and the rewards are well worth the effort.

First, no matter what time you currently wake up, set your alarm 30 minutes earlier. Put your alarm clock across the room and set the volume high enough that you will not miss the buzzer. With the clock across the room, you are forced to get out of bed to shut off the alarm. Once you're out of bed, stay out of bed. In fact, unless your bedfellow is still soundly sleeping, immediately make your bed so as to remove the distraction from your morning and avoid the temptation to crawl back under the covers.

Next, get yourself completely ready to go to work, down to putting on your shoes. This may include your shower, getting dressed, makeup, lunch, and getting together any documents you may need to have with you that day. Put your bag, purse, jacket, and other things you will bring with you, next to your front door so you won't forget them and waste time returning to the house later. Don't leave any stone unturned—be ready to walk out the door at the exact moment you need to leave to arrive at the office on time. After a week or two this will become routine and you will zip through this process quickly without even thinking about what you need to do to be ready to walk out the door.

Next, look at the clock. Notice anything different? Ah, yes. You are ready to go but you have 30 extra minutes staring back at you. No, don't go back to bed. And, no, don't turn on the morning news. Prepare yourself a good breakfast—fresh fruit, eggs or cheese, whole grains, green tea. Instead of inhaling it *en route* to the office, sit down and eat it at a normal pace. But this time, presuming you have no other morning distractions at this hour, turn on your computer and check into your classes. Prioritize these precious moments as follows:

- Determine whether you have anything due by the end of the day in any class;
  - If so, write it down and, if you have time, start working on it.
- Determine if you need to have any readings completed before you can complete your assignments that day;
  - If so, grab the correct book (unless it is an e-book) and place it in your bag for work so that you can read it on a break or over lunch.
- If you have no assignments due, check into your discussion thread and, if you feel prepared, respond to a colleague's posting. Don't formulate your substantive response to the main discussion question in a rush.

What to Eat?

In the morning, you need high-energy and protein to keep you going strong so that you can knock-out those challenging and pesky tasks waiting for you at work. Try instead a breakfast that is both healthy and energizing. You may want to have the ingredients for two or three of your favorite breakfasts on hand at all times so you don't waste time figuring out what to eat each morning. Your breakfast might include a combination of the following:

- Fresh juice
- Bowl of fresh, natural fruit (berries, bananas, mangoes, kiwi)
- Granola (all-natural) with yogurt (or soy yogurt to avoid lactose)
- Eggs (boiled or scrambled)
- DO NOT EAT high-sugar items, like sugary cereals, donuts, pop-tarts. These will cause your body to crash halfway through the morning when you are just getting going on your important work. They also contribute to obesity and diseases like diabetes that can reduce your ability to take advantage of your new education.

A wise investment to facilitate your organization is the purchase of sticky (Post-it) notes. These are ideal for jotting down ideas, reminders, and making lists of things that you need to do, whether it is groceries that you need to buy after work, people you need to call in the next few days, or tasks that you want to accomplish before bed that evening. Consider using different color notes for different things—purple for personal affairs like sporting events for your children and groceries; blue for business affairs like conference calls, network lunches, and résumé workshops; and so forth. Keep a few stacks of sticky notes with you wherever you go (and a few to your planner or calendar that you carry around) and don't forget to review them often. If you have a smart phone, you can also use it to take notes throughout the day. You can use different colored fonts for different tasks. Just be sure to keep a back-up of your notes in case you accidently lose your phone or drop it in the kitchen sink. You may want to experiment with taking notes the old-fashioned and high-tech ways. Many students find that they actually prefer using pen and paper to help them stay organized.

What you have just done with this morning revision is added 30 minutes of productive time and organization to your day. You have eliminated the need to rush through breakfast while driving or settling in to your office environment. You have eliminated the morning rush by adding a comfortable cushion of time that can also be used to deal with emergencies in the house before you leave. You have had a healthy breakfast that will give you energy for the morning. And you have prepared yourself to stay on top of your classes. As an added bonus, you have made yourself a healthier person, too. Studies consistently show that people who eat breakfast every day are less likely to be overweight or suffer from a variety of diseases. And you did all of this with a simple adjustment of your alarm clock. Good job!

But that's not all you can do with your morning. Let's think about your commute to work. If you live in a city, perhaps you take a train or bus to the office. Even a 10-minute commute can be an opportunity to get ahead in your studies. Instead of using the minutes you have on your commute to listen to music or talk radio or get some extra sleep (presuming you are not the person driving), use them to review your readings for the week. Or, if you are driving, listening to the news, which is a great way to stay on top of current events, which can help you to come up with excellent topics for the research papers you are likely to have to write in your classes. When you get to your destination, be sure to jot down any ideas that come to you right away so that you don't forget.

It is essential to be stimulated on your commute to the office or, if you are working out of your home, on your commute to your home office space. Why is it important to have your mind moving by the time you get your workplace? Because that is when you will focus on your most difficult tasks of the day. Perhaps, you left a serious problem unresolved the day (or week) before that is weighing on you, or you have a crucial meeting coming up soon for which you are not prepared. Close your door, ignore your phone, and get focused so that your work does not impede on your education or your family life. Tackle these uber-challenging issues first, while you have energy and minimal distractions. As the day goes on, your energy will dwindle, your colleagues will dawdle, and you will be less productive. The time to do the hard work is the morning—then, when you spend a few moments networking at the water cooler or having a productive lunch, you will feel less anxious, worried, and distracted about work still left undone and can focus on the moment to make the most of the here-and-now.

Coffee or tea? If you live in a city, you certainly cannot avoid the bombardment of Starbucks and its many competitors. Do you stop in for a cup before arriving at work? Do you take a mid-morning break to walk to the nearest café for a boost of caffeine? If so, then you have just discovered another chunk of time in your morning that you can restructure. The best solution is to avoid tea or coffee altogether—it can get expensive and the caffeine can be harder on your body than nicotine. But, if you can't give it up, try switching to green tea or decaffeinated (or "half-caff") coffee to go easy on your body.

Some of us simply can't get through the day without a caffeine boost. If you fall into this category, there are still steps you can take to save time. Consider the amount of time it takes you to go to the coffee shop in the morning. You leave your office, walk to the café, wait in line, order, wait for your drink, perhaps chat with colleagues, and walk back. On a good day, that might be 10 minutes. That is at least 50 minutes per week that you spend getting coffee in the morning. How can you reclaim this time? Consider joining or starting a coffee club in your office where you can have ready-made coffee steps away from your space. Or try bringing a coffeemaker to your office and preparing your own pot each morning. Alternately, you could try preparing the coffee or tea in advance at home using the auto-timer function on your coffeemaker (which you can program before you go to bed the night before). All of these tips can save you time and money and help you focus on more important things.

Summary of morning tips and tricks:
- Add time to your day by advancing your alarm clock
- Eat a healthy breakfast
- Use morning silence for daily preparation
- Make your commute productive and enjoyable
- Tackle the tough tasks first thing in the morning
- Make your own coffee or tea.

5.3 SECTION 2: LUNCH TIME

There is nothing quite like kicking back and chatting with coworkers in the lunchroom or at a local restaurant on your lunch break. It is great to catch up on the latest happenings in their lives and share gossip about your friends and colleagues. That's why it will be particularly difficult for many people to swallow our next piece of advice—eat alone, at least most days. Yes, this sounds antisocial and, in fact, it really is. But this is a significant portion of time in your day that you should take every opportunity to maximize. You will have plenty of time to chat with your friends once your degree is complete and you have moved into the corner office.

To make the most of your lunch time, we suggest a few changes. First, try bringing your lunch with you to work every day. If you simply cannot conveniently bring a lunch with you, find a nearby place where you can buy your lunch to go and take it back to your office with you. I suggest reserving the latter option for days on which you will use your lunch hour to network (discussed below). If you still find your mornings rushed (even after making the changes mentioned in Section 1), consider making your lunch the night before. Putting together a salad or sandwich that you can stow in the fridge until the following morning adds valuable minutes to your day. If your office has a kitchen, you may also consider storing sandwich or salad supplies there and making a quick lunch on site. You may want to keep some basic items at work to make lunch there. You can also keep a week's worth of healthy, frozen entrees in the office freezer if one is available to you.

Second, either eat your lunch at your desk or in a quiet place. Your food should become secondary to the valuable gift of time that you have been given. There are two things you should focus on with your lunch break, and we suggest that you alternate between the two:

1. Stay caught up with your classes. This can include completing your readings, researching online to get a better grasp of the topic that week, completing assignments or discussions, or simply checking ahead to see what you should be working on to get through the class successfully (e.g., final projects or exams).
2. Focus on your career enhancement. Your classes are already enhancing your career, but there is more you should be doing (also see Chapter 10). You can work on cleaning-up your résumé, attending a webinar or reading a research article in your area of expertise, or jotting down your career goals to help keep you focused.

Of course, it would be more fun to read the latest sports scores, chat with a friend, or watch television in the lunchroom. But that is wasted time that you will never get back and that will not move you forward in your professional development. After all, isn't that why you're paying for an education? If you want to be productive and advance your career, those things will have to wait. The key here is to remember that this is a time during your day that should be reprogrammed as a productive, rather than a social period. Free time should be used to help you reach your goals. There is a lot of competition out there for good jobs, and every extra minute spend on schoolwork is an extra advantage you are giving yourself. Remember that you will have some down-time, such as a break between classes and weeks when your workload is not very heavy. You can take advantage of these times to have lunch with friends and catch up on what is happening on your favorite show.

If you have a laptop or iPad, consider bringing it with you to the office in your bag (assuming it will be secure). This will enable you to get some non-office-related work done on your breaks. In some offices in which you are supplied with a work computer, office policy may permit you to use the work computer for personal things when you are not on office hours. This can be invaluable in getting "work done after work." Before trying this, be sure to review your office policy.

Third, reserve some days for networking lunches. Perhaps you would like to talk with a colleague in another department about job openings or career opportunities in that department. Perhaps you want to learn about another field by meeting with someone currently working in that field and asking questions. Or, perhaps you want to speak with a mentor to develop your own career development ideas. Some of your lunch hours should be reserved for these activities as well, as they can be both motivating and uplifting in the middle of your day. If you can, schedule these at locations some distance away from your work to avoid running into colleagues or friends that might make the network aspect somewhat less professional.

At your network lunches, if you plan to meet with a connection that you don't know very well, here are some questions that you may want to use to drive the conversation:

- "Tell me a little bit about what your day at the office looks like."
- "What do you find most rewarding about what you do?"
- "What did you do to prepare yourself for the job that you have now?"
- "Does your job allow you time or opportunities to focus on your professional development?"

Finally, work smarter! Limiting distractions, making every minute count, and completing your tough tasks in the morning will help you get on top of your tasks for sure. But, in addition to organizing your time effectively, you need to use that time in more productive ways. You will learn some technology shortcuts throughout this book, but the lesson here is simple: identify efficiencies that will reduce the amount of time you spend on common tasks. Some examples of what we mean are below:

- Don't wait in line for lunch or coffee. Figure out when peak hours are and avoid those. If you plan to buy your lunch or coffee out (despite my earlier advice), go when it is slow—you will save time and avoid the headache of waiting in a long line when you are hungry or thirsty. The same applies to trips to the post office (don't go at noon!) or other menial tasks.
- Put aside most social networking sites, tweets, and blogs, and instead use your free moments to review your daily task list, update your calendar, or send a professional e-mail. I say "most" because some sites are geared toward professional communication and may not be as wasteful as others.

5.4 SECTION 3: AFTER WORK

You've wrapped-up your day at the office and you're on your way home—exhausted. Or are you? Do you attend happy hours after work? Meet friends for dinner? Consider reserving these events for your weekend and times when your workload at school is lighter. The hours after work constitute the largest single chuck of time that you will find available in your day, and reprogramming that time will, more than anything else, open new frontiers for you.

First, calculate how much time you have between your arrival home and your desired bedtime. Remember that you should try to get between five and seven hours of sleep to be fully functional, so adjust your schedule accordingly. Now, make a list of the things that you need to do each evening before you close-out the day. Do you have to make dinner? Do you want to spend quality time with your spouse and children? Do you have to clean or fix things around the house that can't wait until the weekend? Do you have to wrap-up your course assignments before the end of the day? Call this your essential activity list.

Second, consider the additional things that you do with your evening. Do you watch television? Do you chat online or on the phone with friends? Do you surf the Internet? Do you read novels or magazines? Make a list of these activities in which you participate each week. Call this your entertainment list.

Now is an ideal time to consider your priorities. The list of essential activities that you made will not be easy to change. However, the list of entertainment activities has a great deal of inherent flexibility.

Next, cut the fat. How badly do you need to watch the next episode of "Lost"? How important is it to update your status on Facebook? How valuable is it to you to watch sports highlights or catch an evening game? Do you need to make a different dinner every night, or can your family live with eating leftovers once or twice a week? All of these things are distractions that, while enjoyable, deter us from our education and professional development goals. They take large amounts of time away from us and often give us little in return. The entertainment value is short-lived and will not further our success. In fact, given the trend toward employers researching potential employees on social networking sites, some of these activities could even hurt your prospects of enhancing your career.

Yet replacing these activities with productive activities is not an even exchange. You are exhausted from work. You are no longer in your office environment. And you are now within several feet of all of the temptations of home. How can you possibly maintain focus on anything substantive from this vantage point? Well, there are a few ways to accomplish this.

Do you have a home office? If so, this should be the center of your productivity. If not, do you have the space in your house to set aside a corner for your work? This space should be as far away as possible from the television and kitchen area, where you can concentrate. Invest in a desk and chair and, if you can, a laptop computer to have on the desk. Use this as your physical launching pad from where you will successfully achieve many of your goals. Here is where you can complete your coursework, research career opportunities, complete job applications, attend online webinars and classes, complete papers, draft professional e-mails and letters, and keep records of your progress. This is the center of your professional development.

If you don't have space in the house for this, consider investing in a laptop with a wireless networking card and finding a public library or quiet local café where you can go in the evenings. You might want to pass by the library or café on your way home from work to get your professional development work done before setting foot in the house and facing temptations. Consider this part of your workday but the best part. This is your chance to get ahead in your classes, identify your goals, set an agenda to achieve those goals, and take the steps necessary to accomplish each one. Without a doubt, this will be the formative process in your restructuring and in securing the future you want for yourself.

Be flexible with your restructuring in the evenings. If you have children, you may want to spend the first portion of your evening with them before they go to bed. In this case, your best time to be productive may be after they've gone to bed. If you have to stay late at the office or you have a commitment after work, do your best to maintain your professional development hours or make them up on the weekend.

If you have family obligations, you should also talk with your family members about how you can find some additional time for schoolwork without having a big impact on the family. Perhaps your spouse can take responsibility for dinner or getting the kids ready for bed once a week. You may also want to look closely at your budget to see if you can find a way to pay for things that might make your life simpler and free up time, such as ordering takeout or occasionally using a laundry or cleaning service to free up time.

5.5 CONCLUDING THOUGHTS

We are surrounded today by distractions—television, social networking, happy hours, and instant messaging. As we continue to express a desire to expand our opportunities yet complain of less time to do so, we should consider the value of keeping these distractions in our lives. The professional growth that results from Facebook or the latest reality show is nonexistent. Learning how to restructure our time by eliminating these distractions will undoubtedly change your life forever. You will be smarter, healthier, and more prepared to face the challenges that life throws at you. So now, go forth and cut the fat in your life to make yourself a lighter, happier, and more successful person.

CHAPTER 6

How to Approach Classwork to Maximize Your Chances of Success

Ellie reads all the course material. She knows she understands the material because her professor usually praises her for her discussion board posts. However, she finds herself getting Bs and Cs on weekly quizzes. She is not happy with her quiz grades but isn't sure what she can do to improve her performance.

6.1 INTRODUCTION

Online learning poses unique challenges for students in assessing their classroom performance. While in a traditional school, a student can garner immediate feedback from their contributions to discussions in the classroom and marks on their tests and papers, and can interact live with the professor about their performance, online experiences are not always as transparent. Meeting the requirements for participation may differ significantly from the requirements of an A paper. And when performance suffers, as evidenced by quiz and paper grades, for instance, the online environment may not at first seem conducive to using collaboration to improve; however, nothing could be further from the truth. This chapter will introduce some of the ways in which online collaboration can lead to better performance in the classroom.

6.2 STUDY GROUPS

The first step in forming a study group is to identify classmates who, like you, are smart, motivated, and driven to succeed. By the time the first week is over, you should have read all of your classmates' posts to the first week's discussion board. By doing so you will have a good idea of who has a good grasp of the material, who writes well, and who has taken the time to be careful with their work. There will likely be only a few students who really stand out—these are the individuals you want in your study group.

Once you have identified the people you would like in your study group, the next step is to reach out to them. You should e-mail the individuals you are interested in having in your study group to ask them if they are interested. Include your personal e-mail address and telephone number so that they can easily contact you. If none of the classmates you contact are interested in joining your group, you may want to reach out to the entire class to see if anyone is interested in forming a study group. You should be able to do this via the student café or by sending an e-mail to everyone in class asking if anyone would like to form a study group.

After you have formed your study group, the next step is to figure out how to divide tasks. There is wide variation in how this can be done. Each study group will look a little different based upon what the members of the group hope to achieve by being in the group. However, below are a few ideas on how yours might take shape.

The "divide and conquer model" attempts to partition an otherwise immense load of learning between study group members. Each member of the group will be responsible for developing study guides for the course material. If you choose this model, each member of the study group completes each week's reading individually, but the responsibility for creating a study guide or outline for each week's material rotates among study group members. Study guides or outlines are very useful for reviewing material for quizzes, exams, and tracking how each week's material builds upon itself. They should include outlines of the readings, key points raised by each, and a list of key references or resources in case the student wants to dig deeper into a particular issue. Study guides should be brief and cover only the major points of each week's material. A study guide of 1—2 pages per week should be sufficient for each unit. This is a great model for those students who prefer to work independently but who feel overwhelmed at the amount of work they would need to do to stay on top of the class.

The "collaboration model" focuses on the power and knowledge that emanates from groups of students with diverse approaches to a subject. This approach uses group meetings at prearranged times, whether via instant messaging, video chats, or telephone. During these meetings, members of the group can review the week's material, share ideas for discussion board posts or assignments, or ask questions about material with which you may be struggling. This is a great approach for those students who benefit from hearing the interpretations of others and who build confidence in their knowledge by confirming it with other students.

With any model you choose, there are a few things you should do to ensure that you have a successful group experience. Here are some of those ideas:

1. Limit the size of your group. Once word gets out about your group you may be approached by students wishing to join. An ideal size for a study group is between three and five students.
2. Choose the smartest and most motivated students for your study group—not the students you like the most. The goal of your study group is to maximize your chances for success in class. Although many friendships are formed out of study groups, time spent with your study group should be focused on learning; not on socializing.
3. Remain cordial. Although you may not be in a study group with your friends, you should always remember that your study group formed to work together to maximize each group member's chances of success. Some group members may feel that they are in a competition with one another, and you may need to remind yourselves that you are all in this together. In every online school at which we have taught, there is no requirement that the number of As be limited—you can all share the winner's circle. Nothing makes us feel happier as professors to have a large number of students prove they have mastered the material we taught them by earning As.
4. Set clear rules at the beginning. If you choose to rotate responsibility for creating study guides or outlines, make sure the group's expectations for content as well as the deadline for delivering the completed document to the study group are clear. If your study group is setting up times to meet, be certain that times and dates are set in advance and that expectations for attending the meetings are clear. For example, your group should decide if it is acceptable to miss more than one meeting.
5. Decide on consequences. The consequences for violating study group rules should be decided in advance. If a study group member will be removed from the group if they deliver a study guide late or miss too many meetings, this should be decided in advance. Your group will not want to waste valuable time later on discussing what to do if a group member violates the group's rules.

6. Remember that all work must be your own. Many study groups collaborate closely to ensure that they understand all of the week's material. While it is perfectly acceptable to discuss course material with your classmates and to share outlines with one another, always remember that any work you submit must be yours and yours alone. Under no circumstances should study group members write discussion board posts or papers for each other.

6.3 STUDYING FOR TESTS

Some classes have weekly quizzes while others have mid-term and final exams (some have all of these!). Although the frequency with which you will need to take tests will vary, you will definitely be required to take tests during your time in school. There are several steps you can take to help ensure you do well on these assessments:

1. Keep current with course material. Your professor will create test questions based upon the required material presented in class. This includes required readings as well as lectures, web sites, and other material presented by your professor. If you fall behind in your review of this material, you will spend the time before a test cramming to catch-up rather than studying the material. Don't assume anything in the syllabus or course units is off limits.
2. Take notes throughout the class. As you go through the required course material each week, you should take notes. Your notes should cover the main points covered in the course reading and other course material. When you have a quiz, you can use your notes as a study guide to refresh your memory of past course material. If your test is open book, you can reference your notes during the exam. This is much more efficient that having to look through an entire textbook to find the answer to a question. On timed exams, the time savings this represents may make the difference between an A and B.
3. Create a practice test. Tests can vary widely in their format from one short essay question to 50 multiple choice questions. If the format of the tests is not provided in the course syllabus, ask your professor what to expect. Once you know the format of the test, create practice test questions in the same format. If the test will contain true/false questions, create your own true/false questions. If the test will contain fill-in-the-blank questions, create fill-in-the-blank questions. Use your notes to create questions that you think are likely

to be on the exam. Then, take the exam you created. If the exam will be timed, time yourself taking your practice exam. If you are a member of a study group, each member of the group can create practice questions that can be shared with the group.

4. Ensure that you have sufficient time and no distractions before taking the test. One of the great advantages of taking classes online is that most work can be done at your convenience. The same is usually true of tests and quizzes. Be sure to take your test at a time when you know you will not be interrupted. Some tests may last as long as two or three hours, and it is essential that you have a solid block of time in which to complete your test. Be sure to take your test at a time when you are not likely to be interrupted and you will be able to work in a quiet environment. Many online students find they do well studying while their children play in another room or in a break room during lunch. However, unlike other types of assignments, tests usually have time constraints and you will usually not be given a second chance to take a test even if you did not have time to finish taking it.

6.4 REVIEWING MATERIAL METHOD (FLASHCARDS/ RECORDING)

Regularly reviewing course materials can help you retain what you have learned in class not only throughout the term but also well after class ends. It is not a wise use of time to reread "raw" course material, so you should develop a system of taking notes to keep track of the major themes covered in class. There are several ways in which this can be accomplished. You may want to try different methods of taking notes for review to determine which system works best for you. You may find that just the process of recording important material will help you remember what you have covered in class.

1. Study guides: Study guides are brief summaries of the course material that you build upon each week. In creating a study guide, you should begin the first week of class by writing down the main points covered. You should add to the study guide weekly by continuing to write down the main points covered as the course progresses. Study guides are usually written in narrative form with no more than a paragraph for each point covered. No more than 1–2 pages should be added to the study guide each week. An example of an entry in a study guide might be "Civil rights are individual rights granted to

citizens and are guaranteed by the Constitution. Examples of civil rights are the right to privacy and the right to be free from discrimination. Civil rights are guaranteed by the Constitution."

2. Outlines: Outlines are very similar to study guides, except that instead of creating review notes as a narrative, summary notes are created in list form. Some people find it easier to review material presented in a list rather than as a statement. Just be sure you don't err on the side of being too simple so that you lack any context; include a few details to remind yourself of why you listed each point.

The basic form of an outline looks like this:

Topic or thesis: State your topic or thesis in one or two sentences.

    I. First Broad topic
        A. Subtopic
        B. Subtopic
            1. support (from your research)
            2. support (from your research)
    II. Second Broad topic
        A. Subtopic
            1. support (from your research)
            2. support (from your research)
        B. Subtopic
        C. Subtopic
    III. Third Broad topic
        A. Subtopic
        B. Subtopic
        C. Subtopic

An example is:

Topic: Why It Is Important to Go to the Doctor

    I. Preventive care
        A. Regular check-ups
        B. Ensure immunizations are up-to-date
        C. Ask health-related questions
            1. Review diet and nutrition
            2. Get advice about vitamins and other supplements
    II. Obtain care when sick
        A. Get correct diagnosis
        B. Get prescription if needed

3. Recording summaries: Some people learn better by hearing rather than seeing. If you remember material that you hear in a lecture

better than you remember material that you read in a book, consider making a recording of your review notes. Recorded review notes are also good for those who spend a lot of time in the car. Time spent driving is often unproductive, but this can be an ideal time to listen to recordings you have made related to your course. One disadvantage of recording notes is that it is difficult to go back and edit your recordings, but depending on how you best learn and your schedule, this minor disadvantage should not stop you from recording review notes. Most computers and many phones have the ability to record notes. Mini-recorders that fit in your pocket are also available for reasonable prices. If you record review notes, your notes will be in narrative form very similar to those created in a study guide. The only difference is that you will listen to your notes rather than read them for review. Note that you can sometime complement your studies with already recorded audio files about the subject. A simple Internet search should yield plenty of MP3s (and maybe some videos) discussing the subject you are studying. These are great ways to deepen your knowledge of the area and to prepare you to write papers or essays on point.

4. Flashcards: Flashcards are made using notecards with a concept or term written on one side and additional information about the concept or term written on the other side. Because flashcards are so small you can take them with you anywhere. Because each card contains only a small amount of material, they can be reviewed in even the shortest amount of free time, such as waiting for the bus or waiting to pick your son up from soccer practice. Flashcards are also ideal for classes in which you are learning a lot of new terms because each term can be recorded on a different flashcard. Below is one example of what two flashcards might look like:

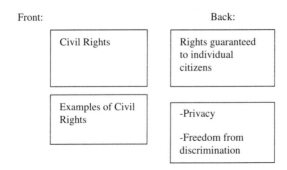

6.5 WRITING GOOD DISCUSSION BOARD POSTS

Nearly all online courses will have discussion board posts as a weekly requirement. A majority of your writing in class may be completed on discussion boards, so it is important that you write your posts well to get the best grade possible. Discussion board posts are also viewable by everyone in class, so it is important that your work appear professional and polished to make the best impression possible on not just your professor but the classmates on whom you may want to rely as study partners and potential job leads.

Professors are usually clear about the basic requirements for discussion board postings. Your professor should tell you how many posts you are required to make each week, how many days per week you are required to post, and approximately how many words each post should be. For example, your professor may require you to post an "original" response to the discussion question for the week and to respond to at least two classmates and specify that responses should be a minimum of 250 words each. Your professor may further require you to post on at least two different days during the week. Be sure that you read and understand these requirements carefully. You may write the best response in class to the discussion question but if you did not post on two different days of the week you still will not receive a perfect score.

After you understand the basic posting requirements, be certain to read the discussion question carefully to be sure you know what is being asked. Some students write excellent discussion board posts that relate to the topic being studied that week, but fail to address the question being asked. Do not fall into this trap. You should read the discussion question *before* you being reviewing the week's material so that you can begin formulating your response as you progress through the week's reading. Don't assume that what other students are writing is correct—stick to the question asked and come up with your own answer. We have taught classes in which the first student to post puts incorrect information in his or her response and the next several students to post repeat the misinformation. While it can be helpful to review what other students have written, always make sure the information you put in your post is correct.

The first post you make to the discussion board each week will likely be your "original" response to the discussion question. This is where you can demonstrate your mastery of the week's material. You should not just regurgitate the material your professor has provided you for the week but should demonstrate your ability to analyze and apply the material. One way to do this is by performing research to find recent events dealing with the week's material. If you have a relevant real-world experience you can share, that is even better, but be sure to relate your experience to the week's readings and do not rely on your experience alone. For example, if you are studying incarceration rates in the United States, you can find out the rate of incarceration in your community and discuss the factors leading to incarceration. If you have a friend or family member who is incarcerated, you can discuss the factors you believe led to the incarceration in the same post in which you share your research. Be sure to cite your references in your posting to avoid a charge of plagiarism.

After you make your initial post to the discussion board, you will likely be required to respond to at least two of the original responses made by your classmates. These posts should not be simply "good point" or "I agree." Rather, your responses to classmates should contain substantive thought that helps move the discussion forward and, if possible, contain information that has not yet been discussed. If you agree with your colleagues' posting, it is perfectly fine to say so. However, you will explain why you agree and add some new material that supports your classmate's point. For example, if you agree with a classmate who states that all defendants in criminal cases should be required to serve jail time after three convictions, discuss advantages to this policy that your classmate has not mentioned and provide references for additional reading on the subject. This type of post will carry more weight than one that just says "I think so, too."

Of course, you will not always agree with your classmates' points of view. Some classes discuss controversial topics such as abortion and the right to own guns. Disagreement on discussion boards makes for an interesting discussion, and most professors will encourage lively debate. However, it is important that you remain polite and stick to the facts, no matter how strongly you disagree with what a classmate has written. Posts that are rude, insulting, or offensive are likely to be removed by your professor and may subject you to disciplinary action. Rather than writing "You are an idiot for thinking incarceration rates are too low," you can write something along the lines of "I disagree with your statement that incarceration rates are too low because in my community nearly 20% of African-American men are incarcerated. Many of these individuals have been incarcerated due to mandatory minimum sentences for relatively harmless crimes in which no one was harmed."

Before posting anything to the discussion board, you should carefully proofread your work. Your post may contain insightful thoughts but if your posts contain spelling and grammatical errors, you are likely to lose points and may even be ignored by classmates who cannot easily digest what you are trying to say. When proofreading be sure that you have properly cited to any sources you used, including the course text. A wise habit would be to draft your response in a word processing program so that you can check for spelling and grammar errors before posting, and so that you can keep a record of your postings should you want to refer back to them in the future.

Finally, you should carefully review all feedback given by your professor to discussion board posts. Your professor is likely to leave feedback specific to your work along with your grade, and you can incorporate his feedback into your next post. Many professors will also post comments to the discussion board itself. If your professor notes that certain posts are well written or insightful, pay attention and learn what your professor considers exceptional work. Because most courses contain multiple discussion boards, you will have many opportunities to improve the quality of your posts as your course progresses.

6.6 WRITING GOOD PAPERS

Many online courses will require you to write papers. Papers generally examine a course topic more in-depth than postings to the discussion board. Requirements for papers will vary greatly, with some papers requiring two pages and others requiring 25 pages. Some papers will be on education policy and others on technology used in law offices. However, regardless of how long your paper is and no matter what the topic is, there are some key points to keep in mind that will help you write a good paper of any length on any topic.

Before you begin writing a paper, you should review the assignment instructions carefully. Be certain you understand the requirements for the paper, including the page requirement and any other details specified such as font style and size. This may not seem very important, but many professors will look for these details to show that you pay attention to detail and may deduct points if you use a font other than the one specified. If your professor has developed a grading rubric, you can often use this as a checklist to ensure that you hit all the key points. Many fields have strict requirements about how written products need to be prepared, and this is good practice for making sure your written works look professional.

For some papers you will be given a specific topic and for others you will be asked to develop your own topic. If you have any questions about a given topic, you should ask your professor to clarify what he or she is looking for well in advance of the paper's due date. If you are asked to develop your own topic, be certain that your topic relates to the course material. For example, if you are taking a class on Business Ethics, a paper on the ethical dilemma posed by stealing a loaf of bread will not be acceptable because it does not relate to business ethics but to a personal ethical dilemma. In contrast, a topic that relates to the ethical dilemma posed by stealing money from a company's coffers is directly related to the topic of the course. When in doubt, e-mail your professor your topic to get his or her input. However, do not ask your professor to come up with a topic for you. If you are stumped, consider looking through online articles in professional journals on the topic, newspapers, and magazines for inspiration. Then, send your initial idea to your professor to ask for his or her feedback and guidance.

Most schools require students to use a specific citation format such as the *Chicago Manual of Style* or the American Psychological Association (APA) style guide. If your school has such a requirement, you should master the requirement early on, as you will use the same citation format in every class and will likely be graded on how well you cite to your sources. If you fail to cite to your sources, you not only will lose points on your paper but risk plagiarism charges that could lead to suspension or dismissal from your program.

It cannot be emphasized enough that everything written in your paper should be your own work. It is not acceptable to merely copy content from a web site or book and present it as your own. It is similarly not acceptable to use long quotes from your sources and simply provide a citation. Your professor is looking for you to demonstrate that you have read *and* understand the material. You can demonstrate your understanding by putting the concepts studied in your own words and providing original examples of how the material can be applied.

As with all written work, it is essential to proofread your paper carefully before you submit it to your professor. You should strive to finish your paper at least a couple of days before it is due. This way, you can set your paper aside for a day, then go back and proofread it after some time has passed. You may be surprised at what you will notice after even just a day away from your paper. If your school has a writing center, you may want to submit your paper for review as well. Keep in mind that most writing centers require approximately 48 hours to review a paper so you will need to plan to have your paper done several days in advance in order to take advantage of this resource. You will likely find the boost you get from the writing center well worth the effort of writing your paper early.

6.7 CONCLUDING THOUGHTS

Remember that everything you write is a permanent reflection of you: how well you understand the material; how well you follow instructions; how well you communicate; and how careful you are. Take care not to submit anything you might find embarrassing if you were to read it in a few months or find it published on a web site. Also keep in mind that anything you write has the potential to be a writing sample you can submit to a potential employer or for admission to a graduate program. In your written submissions, you may not always be right, but you should always do your best. As long as you submit your best work, your professor and your classmates will respect you and your opinion.

CHAPTER 7

Effective Research Techniques in Online Education

Taylor has a great idea for his first paper in his first online class. He sits down and writes about his own experience and interviews his brother to get some more information for his assignment. He's not sure where else to look for information so he goes to Wikipedia. He quotes directly from that web site. He is surprised when his professor returns his paper with a lower grade than he would have liked with the comment that he should have used scholarly sources and avoided opinion.

7.1 INTRODUCTION

Research matters. Whether you are enrolling in your first college-level course or continuing your education following previous degrees, your ability to conduct scholarly research efficiently and effectively is crucial to your success. While you may have a chance to enroll in a course meant to advance your research techniques later in your academic journey, knowing how to find what you need (and what is expected of you) before you start your program can go a long way in helping you stay ahead throughout your studies.

Your ability to conduct effective research is even more important in online education than in traditional education. This is due to the fact that you will have less access to the "hard" resources that a traditional university might have, such as the ability to drop in and ask questions of a research librarian or explore on-site reference books. In an online learning environment, you will be able to access all of the same research resources, but you will have to be more creative in your search for, and utilization, of them. This chapter offers a few insights into how you can leverage online and local resources to enhance your research, develop consistently high-quality references, and impress your professors with the depth and breadth of your sources.

7.2 LEVERAGING LOCAL RESOURCES

No matter where you live, unless you are stationed overseas in a conflict zone, you are likely to have access to a local public library. A local library can be an invaluable source of materials for your research and, in most cases, the librarian in that library is trained to help you find what you are looking for. Become familiar with that library and that librarian, as they will become an important contact for you throughout your entire education experience.

If you do not have a local public library that you can utilize, look for a local college or university. Most of these facilities have their own library and capable librarians. You may run into a problem gaining access if you are not a student at that university. However, if you speak with the librarian or the school's administration office and explain that you are a member of the local community, the school will generally provide you with access. As good stewards of the community, a school is aware of the important role played by the members of their community.

In these libraries, you have access to a plethora of reference resources, including encyclopedias, digests, and other valuable explanatory materials. These materials should be your first stop in learning about a subject for your classes or for a research or writing assignment. Become familiar with the way that the library is organized so that you can easily find the sections of the facility that contain books on topics of interest to you. This way, you can browse those sections frequently and keep your eyes out for new books or books related to that subject (most libraries group books of related subjects close to each other).

If you can't find a book that you need in the library, you may have the option of having the library order it for you from another facility. Many libraries have networks to which they belong and they can utilize those networks to request books from other facilities. If you need a particular book that your library does not carry, ask the librarian if he or she can order a copy from another library. It usually takes only a few days.

Another often overlooked benefit of libraries is their appeal as places for study. Of course, this begins with the golden rule of libraries—silence! Having a quiet environment in which to do your readings for classes, your research for your papers and assignments, and studying for an exam is wonderful when you have an otherwise noisy and distracting environment in the house or at work. Many libraries today even have special areas where you can bring a laptop to do your work while utilizing their high-speed Internet system.

There are other physical benefits of the library that you can utilize. Some libraries have study rooms where you can go to get away from even the traditional library crowd. Making a regular reservation in a room in which you feel comfortable and productive is a great way to stay disciplined and focused in getting your work done on time. It may also be a good place to listen to required lectures or view required videos. Also, some libraries will allow you to set some books aside, either on a vacant shelf or in one of the study rooms. This prevents you from having to lug the books back and forth to home, work, and the library, and it also allows you to keep certain reference books out and ready for you to use. Ask your librarian if these resources are available. They are there to help!

7.3 LEVERAGING ONLINE RESOURCES

As a student in an online educational environment, you probably already have well-developed skills in using the Internet. This will be a big help in finding reference materials online and capturing them using word processing software. In this section, we will discuss how to access professional online resources, how to select the correct resources to apply, and how to integrate those sources into your assignments.

7.4 ACCESSING PROFESSIONAL ONLINE RESOURCES

Even before you enroll in an online course or program, you have probably utilized online databases and search tools. Search engines such as Google and Bing are tools you are likely to have been exposed to, and whether you realize it or not, that exposure has enhanced your research skills. The academic equivalent of these search engines are databases such as EBSCO or Proquest. Typing in a few key words tends to bring you a list of results from which you can select, prioritized either by the relation of the item to the key word or the popularity of the site or document. These skills are useful to start you off on the road to professional research using online resources. Your school's writing center, library, or academic advisor should have more detailed information available for you on how to best and most efficiently use academic search engines.

First, keep in mind that not everything online is considered a professional resource. In fact, open access to many web sites, such as Wikipedia and YouTube, have led to a veritable collection of personal opinions and analyses being passed off as valuable resources. Be wary of these unconfirmed sources as they generally include a level of bias and opinion that make them inappropriate for academic research. Sites such as Wikipedia may be an acceptable place to begin your research, particularly about subjects that are completely unfamiliar to you, but you should never rely on what they say without verifying the information with a scholarly source.

Your focus in online academic research should be on professional sources that provide some or all of the following:

1. Peer-reviewed journal articles
2. Materials from professional associations
3. Books by reputable authors and institutional publishers
4. Materials from government agencies, Congress, and the courts.

Peer-reviewed journal articles are articles written by academics or practitioners that have been subjected to blind review by a panel of experts to assess the validity and value of the article to the field. You can usually trust the reliability of the data in these articles. If you find a journal that contains particularly useful information, you may want to get a subscription for yourself. Student rates are often available.

Professional associations, such as the American Bar Association, the American Medical Association, and the American Red Cross, offer views that are largely reflective of their entire membership and thus can be valuable in establishing a reputable opinion on a particular issue. These should be used carefully, as their views are generally favorable to the interests of their members and their organization, but they should not be dismissed as they tend to provide balanced and well-sourced reviews. For example, the web site of the National Rifle Association and that of the Brady Center to Prevent Gun Violence will have very different views on the topic of gun control and may present the same information very differently; so if you use one of them, try to find the other side to balance out your research, regardless of what your opinion on the issue might be.

Books published by institutional authors, such as university presses, generally offer reputable material. However, always research the author to assess their credentials before relying heavily on a book. A quick Google search of the author's name is a good way to start. If they teach for a university, find out what they teach and make sure that they have some expertise in the area of the book. Almost anyone can publish a book nowadays, and there is no oversight to ensure that the information being conveyed is accurate or reliable. So be cautious and always investigate the author. Don't take any work at face value.

Materials from government agencies are generally reliable. In many cases, if you are looking for data that would be captured by a government agency, the agency itself is the first place that you should go to get it. For example, if you are looking for statistics on water pollution, look to the Environmental Protection Agency. For labor data, reference the Department of Labor. If you have trouble accessing data from an agency, you can pursue a request under the Freedom of Information Act (FOIA), which requires government agencies to disclose most data to the public (http://www.foia.gov/). The same reliability can be placed in materials from Congress, such as legislative histories and reports; courts, such as cases; and regional and international organizations, such as the United Nations and the Organization of American States.

One great resource in the category of government agencies that is often overlooked is the Congressional Research Service, which functions as an arm of the US Library of Congress. They produce reports on a variety of subjects of national interest from immigration to Middle East policy. You can access all of these reports free of charge online through the Library of Congress web site.

In order to ensure that you are accessing the best possible online research materials, start by using professional databases and search engines. Here are a few that you can start with and that you will likely have access to through your online university library:

- LexisNexis (legal and business materials)
- EBSCO (social science materials)
- Proquest (social science materials)
- Westlaw (legal materials)

- Google Scholar (all materials)
- JSTOR (mostly social science journals).

As soon as you have access to your university's online library, find out which databases they subscribe to. Because these universities usually lack a physical library, they make up for it with wide-ranging subscription services that give students excellent access to all the materials they might need in their research. Become familiar with each database and how it works to ensure that when the time comes for you to utilize it, you won't spend hours in tutorials or e-mailing your students and professor with questions that you can easily answer in advance. If there is a particular database you were hoping for that is not on your school's list, contact the reference librarian. There may be an equivalent database to which they do offer access, or there may be a way that you can gain access through other means.

When performing Internet research, always be aware of the end of the Internet address or the top-level domain. Common domains are .org, .com, .edu, .gov, and .mil. If a web site ends in .org, that site is maintained by an organization. If this is the case, you should investigate the organization further to see if you can rely on their site. Keep in mind that the data there will likely be biased toward the interests of that organization. If a web site ends in .edu, that site is maintained by an educational institution. Web sites maintained by educational institutions often contain useful and interesting information, including current research being performed by professors and doctoral students. However, you should also be skeptical of this information, as it may express a certain viewpoint espoused by the academic institution or the author. Some academic work is reviewed by others in the field through the peer review process. If you know that work has been peer-reviewed, it carries more weight as a body of experts has provided their unbiased review of the work.

If a web site ends in .gov, it is maintained by a government agency, which could be federal, state, or local. Sites that end in .gov usually contain recent and reliable information, and they often provide sufficient information about the sources of any data that they present. Sites that end in .mil are maintained by the military. Because these sites are maintained by a governmental source as well, they are usually accurate, reliable, and current.

Sites that end in .com are usually run by for-profit companies. Many of these sites may contain useful information, but you should be skeptical of any information found on these sites as there is no independent review of the material and no legal requirement that they present only factual information. Some commercial sites may have the look and feel of government sites, but are not—so be sure to check the web address before getting too far along in your research.

You may also come across sites that end in .jp, .fr, or .uk. If you see a web address that ends in what appear to be random letters, it probably indicates that the web site is maintained in a foreign country. In the examples here, the countries that maintain the sites are Japan, France, and the United Kingdom. Unless you are accessing government or academic sources from overseas, be wary of any information posted on a site maintained in a foreign country. You may find a great web site discussing employment law in detail, but if you discover it ends in .uk, much of what you find on the site may be irrelevant to the paper you are writing on employment discrimination in the United States.

The Internet is likely to be the single best source of information for your academic research, so you should indeed leverage it as a central tool in your work. Just bear in mind the tips above as you do so. You don't want to end up criticized because you failed to confirm your sources. Just remember what happened in China recently:

> *The Chinese Communist Party's official mouthpiece apparently fell for a parody by The Onion, the satirical newspaper and Web site, when it reported…that Kim Jong-un, the young, chubby North Korean ruler, had been named the "Sexiest Man Alive for 2012."* [1]

7.5 SELECTING THE CORRECT SOURCES TO INCLUDE

Now that you know where to find valuable research sources, you need to know how to use the material in your assignments and discussions properly. It doesn't take much effort to select a single source that says what you want to say and attach it to your document. That is the reason single sources are not preferred in scholarly writing. Your goal

[1] http://www.nytimes.com/2012/11/28/world/asia/chinese-news-site-cites-onion-piece-on-kim-jong-un.html

should be using multiple sources and focusing on comparative sources. Moreover, while your class text is an acceptable source, it should never be the only source you use, as your professor will want to see that you acquired additional knowledge through independent research, not just in completing your coursework.

When you begin research for a paper or discussion posting, you should come upon a number of journals, books, and other reputable documents that speak to the topic you searched for. You don't need to integrate each of these into your assignment, but you do need to sift through them to find the best sources. When you use secondary materials, try to prioritize them in this manner:

1. Original research conducted and analyzed by the author
2. Secondary research reviewed and analyzed by the author
3. Reviews of analyses conducted by other authors.

Your best bet for a reputable source is always the author or governmental agency that conducted the study. However, many articles you come across are likely to analyze a study conducted by someone else, making it a secondary source rather than a primary source. The further away you get from the original study, the more room for bias and misinterpretation of the results. Of course, this is not to say that other authors do not have valuable contributions and insights to make to the original study. They should still be utilized; just bear in mind that secondary analyses may misrepresent the original data.

Finding the primary sources is easy. If you have a secondary source in hand, that is, reviewing data from somewhere else, it is standard practice for that author to discuss the original study and to provide a citation to that study. Start your research by going to that original study and reviewing the researcher's own analysis before looking further at secondary analyses. You will be much better prepared to discuss the shortcomings of subsequent analyses after having done this.

If you happen to be doing legal research for one of your classes, make sure that you are always looking for the correct case law and statutes. For cases, if you plan to cite to a specific case, be sure that the opinion (1) is the most recent decision on the case (i.e., make sure you are citing the highest appeal if the case was appealed); (2) has not been overturned or otherwise challenged by a more recent decision of any court; and (3) is the first case to make the statement you are extracting (i.e., if the court is referring to an older opinion, go back and find that opinion to get to the source). For statutes, always check to ensure that the statute has been enacted (i.e., it is not just a Bill or proposal) and that, if it is a state statute, that it applies to the situation you are referring to (i.e., a statute from Nevada would have little or no effect on an act in Pennsylvania).[2]

7.6 INTEGRATING SOURCES INTO YOUR ASSIGNMENTS

When you have all of the sources you feel that you need, the next step is to integrate them into your assignment. This is not simply a matter of adding a footnote here or there for support. Rather, you should be identifying where each source properly fits into your discussion and how it relates to your own analysis.

Each paragraph that you write should begin with a topic sentence. That is generally going to be your own statement of the issue you will address in that sentence. The next two or three sentences will be your analysis in support or contrast to that topic sentence. This is where you should use your reference material. Adding a sentence about how the analysis done by a particular author or group of authors is particularly important in addressing this topic. Is there general agreement on the topic or are there conflicting opinions? Is the topic so new that the jury is out on a final conclusion? Address these in the body of the paragraph utilizing the sources that you found. Your paragraph should conclude with a simple sentence that ties together the topic sentence to the analysis. Below is an example.

> *Organic food is less toxic for the environment than nonorganic food. Numerous authors have found evidence of high levels of toxins in groundwater near where pesticides are used in agriculture (Johnson, 2010; Sanders, 2004; Thomas, 2006). These pesticides were used to protect the produce from pests and disease. However, the resulting toxins in the groundwater have been linked to a higher incidence of cancer among the local population (Smith, 2009). Organic foods, which do not permit the use of pesticides, facilitate less toxic groundwater and safer communities.*

---

[2]For more detailed information about using cases and statutes in your research, consider reading *Narrowing the Gap: Legal English for the New International Legal Practitioner* by Dr. Kevin Fandl, which has valuable and straightforward tips for researching and applying cases in the United States.

As you can see from this sample paragraph, the topic sentence begins the discussion and stimulates interest in the research. The three body sentences offer support for that topic sentence. And the last sentence links the original idea to a conclusion based upon the evidence supplied in the body of the paragraph. If each of your paragraphs are drafted using this same approach, you will have a stronger argument and, very likely, a better grade.

Note that this type of source-based writing will be required for most undergraduate and graduate assignments. Even if the professor does not require a certain number of sources in your assignment, it is wise to err on the side of too many rather than too few academic sources. In some classes, discussion postings also require sources. In these cases, follow the same approach discussed here when presenting your responses to the discussion questions.

It is very important to remember that you must provide a citation anytime you rely upon or use someone else's work or ideas. If you do not do so, you risk plagiarism charges that carry very serious consequences ranging from having to completely redo your assignment or discussion post to expulsion from your program.

7.7 TIPS FOR EFFECTIVE RESEARCH

1. Is Wikipedia a good source? What about other wikis?
   Wikipedia and other wikis, as they have become known, are useful inventions of the digital age. They provide quick access to a variety of information on topics from Abraham Lincoln to zoology. However, the information posted on these sites is largely unverified or, if it is verified, it is not peer-reviewed. Accordingly, it is not wise to use these as a source of information. That does not mean that you should not look to them to get familiar with a topic. The reference list in most entries is good and will lead you to original sources that may speak directly to your topic. Use those references as a useful starting place in your scholarly research, but never cite wikis as academic sources. If your professor sees that you have done so, he or she is likely to deduct points from your grade.
2. Which citation style should I use?

Most, but not all, academic programs today prefer that you follow the style of the American Psychological Association, or APA. APA is a relatively straightforward style to understand, but you should always keep your APA manual nearby to make sure that you are properly formatting your document. If you are unsure of a particular style, you can look online at the Purdue University OWL web site.

Note that if you are doing legal writing for your program, you may be asked to use the Blue Book (*A Uniform System of Citation*) for your style guide. The Blue Book is quite distinct from the APA, so you will benefit from spending time learning about its unique approach to citation.

3. Which database is the best for me?

There is no one answer to this question. Which database is best depends on what you are researching. Most databases that you encounter online have an information tab that tells you the material that you will find inside and the dates of coverage. Make sure that you review this before you begin your research and ask your school librarian if you have questions. Here is a list of some of the more common databases along with what you can find on those sites:

CIAO (Columbia University)—International affairs research

ERIC (Education Resources Information Center)—bibliographic information on journal articles

World Bank Database—data on international development topics

Proquest—full text journal articles, theses, and dissertations

JSTOR—social science full journal articles

LexisNexis—full text legal materials and news items

EBSCO—full text journal articles and business news

4. How do I know when I have researched enough sources?

It is not an easy thing to know when you have enough sources to feel confident that your analysis will be well received. One way to know, especially when researching for major documents such as theses and dissertations, is when you begin to see the same articles referenced as sources in documents that you read. If every new piece that you come across is using the same sources you have already become familiar with, you may have reached a point where you are comfortably confident in your knowledge of the topic. Of course, as data continues to be collected and issues reanalyzed all the time, be sure that your research is always current by doing one last sweep of research materials before you submit your document for review.

5. The assignment doesn't say how many sources I need. What do I do?
Unless you are responding to an assignment that explicitly requests your opinion and nothing else, you should expect to include sources. Even though you may have years of experience in your field, you, like us, are no expert in every topic. But others are, and your use of their analysis and data to support your own analysis will help you significantly strengthen your document, help you become a knowledgeable scholar in this area.

6. Footnotes or in-text citations?
The APA prefers that authors use in-text citations rather than footnotes. However, if you are planning to include explanatory parentheticals, which provide information about a specific point raised in the main text that would not be appropriate to keep in the main text, a footnote is the preferred mechanism to add that material. An example is below:

> In a recent study, a group of scientists argued that drinking sugary beverages directly lead to obesity (AMA, 2012). Their conclusions are based upon data collected over a period of 20 years across the entire United States. And, although the findings are inconclusive,[3] they point to the fact that higher sugar intake leads to more retention of fat beneath the skin.

In the example above, information that is apart from but relevant to the main text is included in a footnote. For those students enrolled in legal studies program in which the Blue Book is the preferred citation approach, footnotes are preferred over in-text citations for most documents. If your school prefers another citation format, be sure that you understand which approach that is before you submit your first written assignment. If you are having trouble with citations, your school's writing center or library should be able to provide you with additional resources.

7. Can I use news articles and opinion pieces as sources?
News articles and opinion pieces are valuable to provide background and insights into a particular issue. They often draw attention to an aspect of an issue that we had not previously considered, which can

---

[3]Several of the scientists in this study admitted that the higher rates of obesity could also be connected to a lack of exercise by study participants.

be helpful in formulating our research questions for theses and dissertations. However, they should not generally be used as sources for your assignments and major papers. There is no third-party verification (peer review) of the articles, making them susceptible to incorrect information, and the opinion pieces are by their very design opinions, so they do not offer an unbiased view of an issue. If you must use a news article as a source, prefer articles from major news media, such as the *New York Times*, *Washington Post*, or periodicals like the *Economist* or *Newsweek*. These publications have reputations that depend on the veracity of information that they print and thus may be more reliable than some smaller news outlets.

8. What is FOIA?

The Freedom of Information Act (FOIA)[4] was enacted in 1966 to allow public access to federal agency records. FOIA allows individuals to submit requests to the government for information that they may have in their files concerning a specific matter. As long as your request is precise enough, you can demand that the federal agency provide you all documents related to your request. Failure of the agency to respond without cause can lead to agency liability and a lawsuit. Most states have similar laws for state agencies. FOIA is one mechanism that researchers may use to acquire data from agencies that otherwise do not make that data publicly available.

You can learn more about how to file a FOIA request here: http://www.foia.gov/.

7.8 CONCLUDING THOUGHTS

Nearly all of your assignments for online classes will involve some amount of research. Finding good sources to integrate into your work is the foundation for your success in written assignments. There is no shortage of credible sources to choose from when conducting your research that you can use to enhance your knowledge of any topic you may encounter along your educational journey. By using the techniques we have taught you here, you will be able to quickly and easily find sources that will help your strengthen your analysis and submit top work.

[4]5 U.S.C. §552 (1966).

CHAPTER 8

Writing for Success

Max writes e-mails all day long at work and is used to a very informal style of writing. He approaches his first discussion board posts the same way and is surprised to find that his grade is not as high as expected.

Tiffany has written plenty of reports and analyses for her office, and no one has ever criticized her work. She follows that same writing style on her first written assignment in her online graduate program. Her professor hands her back a C and tells her that she needs to learn APA writing style before she submits her next paper.

8.1 INTRODUCTION

In all online classes you should expect to submit substantial written work on a weekly basis. In some graduate programs we have taught in, this can be as much as a 5–10 page research paper each week. This is because writing is a necessary substitute for time spent in the classroom interacting face-to-face with your professor and classmates. Writing is how you will establish your presence in class and how you will demonstrate to your professor that you understand the material you are studying and that you know how to carry out proper research and writing assignments, which you will need in most professional careers. You will be expected to develop these research and writing skills through a combination of writing discussion board posts, writing papers, and possibly writing exam essays.

To get the best grade possible on all of your written work, you need to not only understand the material but also able to clearly communicate your understanding of the material through clear and precise writing. The tips below will help you be the best writer you can be—and get the best grade you can. Although the length of your written work will vary based upon course requirements and the type of assignment, the same process should be used for all written work.

8.2 AVOID PLAGIARISM AND SELF-PLAGIARISM

The most important step you can take to ensure that you submit a good assignment, eligible for the highest grade possible, is to ensure that all work you submit is your own and that you provide citations to all sources from which you used information or ideas. If you do not do so, you risk a charge of plagiarism. If you are found to have plagiarized an assignment, the penalties range from having to redo the entire assignment, to failing a class, to expulsion from school. Every school has its own plagiarism policy, which clearly explains what that school considers plagiarism and the consequences of plagiarizing work. Make sure that you know and understand your school's plagiarism policy before you submit your first discussion board post and paper.

As a general guideline, the vast majority of writing needs to be your own and should not have previously been submitted to another class. Although it is acceptable to use some quotations, they need to be clearly indicated with quotation marks and the sources clearly identified. No more than 10% of your paper should contain quotations from other sources. Even if the sources of your quotes are clearly identified, quotes represent someone else's work and your professor will not give you full credit if you do not demonstrate in a substantial way that you understand the material and can explain it in your own words.

You should not submit work that you have done to multiple classes. Even though the work may be your own, this constitutes "self-plagiarism" and is usually subject to the same plagiarism policies as submitting someone else's work as your own. Although it may be tempting to submit a paper you put a lot of effort into for another class, you must demonstrate new learning in each class. Many schools consider it plagiarism if you attempt to submit the same work more than once, since you cannot receive credit for the same work twice.

Many schools submit student work to services such as Turnitin.com that are able to check writing against content available on the Internet sources and against work submitted by students throughout the country at thousands of schools. This includes your own past work as well!

If you are struggling with an assignment for any reason or feel you do not have enough time to write a good paper that is your own work, the answer is *never* to submit someone else's work. Instead, you should reach out to your professor for guidance or additional time to complete your assignment. We have had promising students receive zeros on assignments and fail classes for trying to take shortcuts and using discussion board posts used by their friends in past terms, purchasing papers from online sites, and submitting papers they wrote for other classes. A charge of plagiarism has serious consequences and remains on your record forever. Do not allow this to happen to you.

8.3 PREWRITING STEPS

Before you dive into your assignment, there are some steps you should take to ensure that once you begin writing you fully understand the assignment and know what you are going to write. This will save you a lot of time as you will not find yourself mid-way through writing a response, only to discover that you do not understand a portion of the assignment and need to start over.

8.4 UNDERSTAND THE REQUIREMENTS

Before you begin writing, you should first make sure you clearly understand exactly what the assignment requires, both in terms of substantive content and general formatting requirements such as page length, font, and citation format. You should also be sure that you understand how the assignment will be graded. If the assignment will be graded using a grading rubric, you should review the rubric carefully before you begin to write. If you have any questions at all about any aspect of the assignment, ask your professor before you begin writing. Once you do begin writing, you should be sure to have the assignment instructions and grading rubric in an easily accessible place. Refer to the instructions and grading rubric throughout your writing to ensure that you stay on track from beginning to end. Although this may seem obvious, students sometimes submit posts that go in-depth about a portion of a week's reading that they were not asked to write about on that week's discussion board. No matter how good such posts may be, the student will still receive a poor grade because they did not answer the question being asked. Similarly, students sometimes submit very well-written and well-reasoned papers but still wind up with a poor grade because they did not use the required number of sources or came under the required page limit or word count. With some simple preparation, you can avoid these types of simple mistakes and get the best grade possible.

8.5 KNOW YOUR GOAL

When writing a paper, you should have a clear goal in mind. Before you begin writing you should determine what you want to accomplish. Depending on the type of assignment, your goal will be to Predict, Inform, Persuade, or Explain. An easy way to remember the possible goals of writing is PIPE. After you read the assignment instructions, ask yourself which of these you are being asked to do, or on which part of the PIPE you are being asked to focus, then keep that goal in mind throughout the writing process.

Writing that goal asks you to tell the reader what you expect to happen. These assignments will generally give you a set of facts and ask to tell the reader what you expect to happen. An example of a predictive writing assignment is "Jill struck a boy who darted into the street to catch a ball and the boy died. Jill was driving five miles over the speed limit. Her blood alcohol level was within the legal limit for driving, but showed that she had been drinking. Will Jill be found guilty of murder?" When writing your responses to these assignments, you should not simply offer your prediction but fully explain why you made the prediction you did. There may not be a right answer to the question asked in predictive writing, so it is important that your professor is able to see exactly why you made your prediction. It is also important that you do not give your personal opinion but use the information you have learned in class to make your prediction. In the example given, you would discuss the elements of murder that you would have studied in class or researched. You would then discuss how the lack of time for Jill to stop, her speed, and her blood alcohol level related to the elements of murder to predict whether Jill would be found guilty of murder.

Writing that prediction asks you to educate the reader about a topic. These assignments generally ask you to tell the reader about a topic. An example of an informative assignment is "What is a career in Criminal Justice you would like to pursue?" When writing your response to these assignments, you should not simply give a short answer or provide definitions of terms but fully explain the topic. In the example given, you should write about the career you chose in detail and then explain why it would be a good fit for you. If the assignment requires more information, you could discuss other careers studied in class and explain why those would not be as good a fit for you as the one you choose.

Writing that persuades you to convince the reader about your views on a topic. These assignments generally ask you to give your opinion and then defend your response. An example of a persuasive writing assignment is "What is the best policy for a professor to adopt regarding late assignments?" Again, you would not simply give your personal opinion about the best policy, but provide a reasoned response supported by facts and data. In the example given, you could discuss how a policy that accepts assignments up to a week late without penalty is best. You would support your policy with facts showing that most students who do not submit an assignment on time will submit the assignment within a week of the due date, and that students who do not submit their assignments within a week are not likely to submit the assignment at all. Telling your reader that you think a certain policy is fair is not enough. You must fully explain why this is so and provide factual data to support your opinion.

Writing that asks you to tell the reader how to accomplish a task. These assignments generally ask you to walk the reader through the process of accomplishing a task. These types of assignments are more commonly seen in math, science, and computer science classes but may be seen in other disciplines. An example of a writing assignment that asks you to explain is "How does a snake shed its skin?" In the example given, you would walk the reader through the stages of how a snake sheds its skin step-by-step, beginning with an explanation of how a snake grows its skin and the process it uses to get out of its old skin.

8.6 STAGES OF WRITING

Once you fully understand the assignment's requirements and have identified the goal of the assignment, it is time to put pen to paper or, more likely, fingers to the keyboard. There are some key steps you should take to ensure that your writing is as through and as good as it can be.

First, you should engage in prewriting exercises. You should note the issues, elements, and facts that you want to include in your paper. Keep this list readily available to ensure you do not neglect to include anything in your final paper.

Second, you should review the list you have made and identify any areas which you will need to research. You should review the chapter on research for guidance on how to complete this step. As you conduct your research, remember to stay focused on the topic of your assignment and the goal you have in writing. Note down any relevant information as you find it along with the source.

Third, once you have gathered all of the information you need to begin, you should brainstorm ideas by noting down specific points you may want to include in your paper, such as personal stories or examples, to strengthen your arguments or illustrate the points you are going to make.

Fourth, you should create an outline before you begin writing. Creating an outline will help you organize your paper before you begin writing the detailed information you will need to complete your assignment. By writing an outline you will be able to clearly organize your thoughts and the structure of your paper without being weighted down by the nitty-gritty of your topic. This will save you time and energy in the long run. Be flexible and willing to move things around as you get going with the paper.

To create an outline, you should follow three simple steps: (1) list main topics in a general way; (2) group related ideas and topics together; and (3) arrange material in a logical way. Depending on your own approach to writing, your outline may be general or very detailed. However, once you have completed your outline, you should have the major topics and subtopics of your paper identified and the structure of your paper established.

An outline on how to prepare for a dinner party might look like the one given below:

  I. Introduction
 II. Guests
     a. Choosing invitations
     b. Sending invitations
     c. Keeping track of RSVPs
III. Creating a seating plan
 IV. Planning the menu
     a. Appetizer
     b. Main course
     c. Dessert

V. Serving dinner
VI. Cleaning up
VII. Conclusion

8.7 DRAFTING

Once your outline is complete, it is time to start filling in each major topic and subtopic with substantive information. The drafting stage is where you more fully develop your ideas and analysis. In this stage, you will tie together the issues you have identified with the research you have performed. When completing your draft, you should write in complete sentences as you are getting closer to having a finished product.

8.8 REVISING

The revision step is often overlooked, mainly because many students rush to submit their assignment on time. However, catching small errors at this last stage can show the professor that you put effort into submitting a well-done paper rather than a rushed draft. This step is key to submitting a good finished product. After you have a complete draft, you should review your paper carefully and make revisions. During the drafting stage, you were concerned with ensuring that you included all relevant information. During the revision stage, you will focus on the style of your paper and make revisions to ensure your paper is clear and understandable. If they are not already present, you will revise your paper to insert transition sentences, headings, and the other elements discussed later in the chapter that will move your writing from conveying the basic information necessary to passing as a well-written academic paper. If you discover during the revision process that additional content will make your paper better, you should include that information. Many students reread and revise their paper several times before they consider it complete.

8.9 EDITING

After you have revised your assignment for style and content you are close to being finished—but not quite. You will also need to edit your assignment to ensure you do not have any errors in punctuation, spelling, or grammar and that your paper flows well. While editing you should pay attention to detail. You will be working the paper into its final form. Although not always possible, try to edit your paper no later than 48 hours before your assignment is due. Then, just before you submit your assignment, read it over one last time to ensure you have not missed anything. Developing a good assignment takes time, and giving yourself a 24-hour "break" from an assignment to clear your mind will allow you to look at your assignment with fresh eyes before you turn it in. You may catch some errors that you had not noticed before and give yourself the opportunity to hand in the best product possible.

You can make the editing process easier through the use of tools in recent versions of Microsoft Word. For instance, you can use the highlighter tool to note areas of your papers that you want to confirm before submitting. You can also use track changes to make edits to your papers as you move through the drafting process. It is always a good idea to save versions as you move along, just in case you accidentally delete something that you want to reinsert down the road.

8.10 WRITING TIPS

You now know the stages you need to follow to write the best assignment possible. The tips below will give you an edge on your classmates so that your assignment will be easy to follow. If your writing is clear, your professor will have an easier time determining that you understand the material and you will earn a better grade. Below, we have provided the writing tips that we believe will give you the best opportunity to earn the highest grade. However, there are innumerable other techniques you can use to improve your writing. If you find that you are still struggling with your writing or not earning the grades you would like even after using all of the guidance here, we suggest that you consult your school's writing center or your professor for additional help.

First, you should always start with an introduction. Your introduction should tell the reader what the rest of your assignment will be about. An effective introduction restates what you believe the assignment to be and how you plan to go about addressing it. It draws attention to the unique approach that you will take, if any.

Second, you should use headings to alert the reader to what you are about to discuss in different sections of your assignments. Think of these headers as headlines and put them in bold or underline them (not both—overemphasis reduces the impact of any emphasis). For example, a paper about how to make a pizza would have different sections on the steps involved. The headers might be "Making the Dough; Making the Sauce; Preparing the Toppings; and Baking the Pizza."

Third, you should use transition sentences to tie your paper together and make it easy to read. There are several ways to do this. The most common way is to use transitional words such as "however," "moreover," "therefore," "accordingly," and "further." An example of how to use transitional words is: "Generally, employers are not liable for an employee's misconduct if the misconduct is not related to their job duties. However, there are exceptions to this rule." Another way to transition is to use repetition of term or echo words from sentence to sentence. To do so, you pick up a word/phrase at the end of previous sentence and use the same word/phrase at beginning of next sentence or paragraph. An example of how to echo words to transition is: "Mr. Brown and Mr. Green signed *a contract. The contract* stated that Mr. Brown would sell Mr. Green his car for $10,000." Another option is to transition using demonstrative pronouns followed by a noun. In using this technique of transitioning, words such as "that," "such," "those," and "these" are commonly used. An example is: "The Judge questioned Mr. Brown about his employment. *That* line of questioning elicited Mr. Brown's admission that he had a second job fixing cars at the local service station."

Fourth, in order to avoid plagiarizing others' work, you need to know how to paraphrase what others have written effectively. A paraphrase is your attempt to restate ideas expressed by someone else in a new form and, importantly, in your own words. Paraphrasing is a legitimate way to use information from another source, as long as you provide a citation to the original source. A simple quotation should only be used when someone else makes a point that you simply could not say any better if you paraphrased it or if there is famous quote you want to include. Use these sparingly.

What your professor will be looking for is for you to demonstrate that you understand the material and can use what you have read to express own ideas. Paraphrasing accomplishes this goal and leads to better writing. To paraphrase you should: (1) change the words used; (2) change the structure of the sentence; (3) insert your own ideas;

(4) use quotation marks to identify any phrases you have borrowed directly from the source; and (5) provide a citation to the original source. An example of paraphrasing would be taking the phrase:

It is problematic to define a handicap by providing a list of the types of disabilities that will be covered because certain groups of handicapped people might be excluded. The legislature might simply be unaware of certain handicaps.

And paraphrasing it like this:

The term "handicap" is difficult to define in a statute. (Cite). Any attempt to provide a complete list of covered disabilities, however, will be inadequate; some conditions will inevitably be omitted. (citation).

Fifth, always end with a conclusion. Your conclusion should be a paragraph or less and provide a short summary of what you have written. This will tie together all of the information you have gone over in your written assignment and provide a cue to the reader that your writing is coming to an end rather than leaving the reader hanging.

8.11 CONCLUDING THOUGHTS

By using the process and tips for writing in this chapter, you will position yourself to earn the best grade possible on the many writing assignments you will complete in every class you take online.

CHAPTER 9

Common Pitfalls and How to Avoid Them

Jennifer has had a very busy week at work. She plans to spend all day Sunday working on a major paper that is due on Monday. She looks at the assignment for the first time Sunday morning and finds the assignment confusing. She sends an e-mail to her professor saying "Hi. I started the assignment and am lost. Can you help? She is relieved to see a response in her inbox a few hours later, but when she opens the e-mail she finds the professor has only responded with questions about which assignment she needs help with and asking her to explain with which part of the assignment she is having difficulty. Instead of getting the information she needs, Jennifer has missed an opportunity to get the information she needs before the assignment is due.

Mike knows better, but somehow the term has gotten away from him. With two weeks left to go Mike realizes that he is failing his class. He is too embarrassed to contact his professor and accepts that he is going to fail the class. Instead of moving on to the next class with his classmates, he has to take the failed class over, losing time and money.

9.1 INTRODUCTION

At some point during your educational career you are likely to encounter one or more problems—getting lost in class, having a medical emergency, or not feeling like you have anything to contribute to class. Knowing what kinds of problems are likely to arise and how to avoid them ahead of time will give you a huge advantage over your classmates. In this chapter, we will discuss the most common problems and how to handle them.

9.2 I JUST STARTED SCHOOL AND I DON'T KNOW WHAT I'M DOING

Starting a new school can be overwhelming if you do not take the time to prepare. Once class begins, you want to be able to focus on your studies and not have to worry about administrative details. One of the best ways to avoid feeling lost when you first start school is to gain as much information as possible about the school by attending all available orientation sessions before you begin classes. Orientation sessions will help familiarize you with the university's policies, learning management system, and other resources. This will help you navigate the system easily and put you in the best position for success. Some schools offer a comprehensive orientation, and others offer several orientation sessions on different topics, such as navigating the classroom and how to use the library.

A real-life example of what can happen if you do not attend orientation is that you may start your first class without knowing how to obtain the required course texts. Students in this position find themselves scrambling to find out where to get their books in the first days of class when the majority of their classmates are busy delving into substantive material and posting their first responses to the discussion board.

During orientation, the university will familiarize you with resources that may be available to you, such as a writing center, tutoring services, and a virtual library. Orientation will also provide you with information that you may not need immediately but are likely to need at some point during your schooling, such as how to contact your academic advisor and the financial aid office.

If you have already started school and did not attend orientation sessions, it is not too late. Contact your academic advisor for information on how to attend the next orientation session being offered. If you are so lost you do not know how to contact your academic advisor, reach out to your professor for help.

9.3 MY CLASS JUST STARTED AND I AM ALREADY LOST

Some students start class and fall behind very early in the term. Falling behind early on can create problems that resonate throughout the rest of the class. If you take the time to know what is expected at the outset of each class, and what your professor expects you to do if you fall behind, you can avoid this common pitfall.

All students, whether just beginning their studies or nearing the end of their degree requirements, should take a few minutes at the beginning of every class to review the syllabus, class policies, and any announcements posted by the instructor. If your professor took the time to post something to the classroom, he or she expects you to take the time to read it. Although many universities have standard policies, each professor has different expectations. Your professor will be much more willing to work with you if a problem arises if you demonstrate that you have read and understood all class requirements and expectations. You should not expect your professor to restate posted information for you personally. If you ask your professor how many times you have to post to the discussion board, his or her response will likely be to refer you to the syllabus or posted class policies. This creates a potentially embarrassing situation. Your professor is also likely to be unsympathetic if you lose points in your first weeks of class for not following stated class policies.

For example, do not assume that just because your professor from last term accepted assignments a week late without penalty, that your professor this term will do so. If you are going to ask your professor for an extension, do not ask what is required unless you have reviewed the professor's policy regarding late work. Your professor will be much more willing to work with you if your request shows that you have read and understood the policy. A good request will read like the following: "Per your late policy, I am requesting an extension due to a severe illness. With your prior approval, I will submit assignment #4 one week after the initial due date. I understand that I will be penalized one point per day late." Compare that with a request that reads "I was very busy last week and couldn't get to my paper. I'll send it to you later." Which student do you think the professor is more willing to work with?

9.4 I KEEP LOSING POINTS ON MY ASSIGNMENTS AND I DON'T KNOW WHY

Some students may find that they lose points on assignments due the first week. Other students may do very well the first few weeks of class, then receive a poor grade on their first paper. Lost points may come as a surprise to students who are working hard or who have a history of receiving high grades. If you find yourself in a situation where you are not doing as well as you would like, and you do not know why, there are a few steps you should take.

First, be certain to review all assignment instructions carefully. If you are losing points, you may discover that you are not addressing all portions of the assignment. You may also find that you are not following all of the assignment's instructions regarding how the assignment should be written. For example, some students are so focused on writing their papers that they do not pay attention to the portions of the assignment instructions pertain to the paper's format, such as the professor's preferred font or citation method. If your professor specifies these details, you need to pay attention or risk losing points. You should review the assignment instructions again before submitting your assignment to be sure you have met all of the assignment's requirements.

Second, in addition to providing you with assignment instructions, many professors will also provide you with grading rubric for papers and discussion board postings. The use of grading rubrics is becoming more common at online universities. If your professor uses a grading rubric, you should review the rubric carefully before beginning your assignment. The grading rubric will provide you with valuable insight into the criteria your professor will use to grade your assignment. You may want to go through and try to "grade" your paper using the rubric. If you would not give yourself an A using the grading rubric, you should revise your assignment.

Third, you should take the time to proofread your work carefully. A student who is certain they "aced" an assignment may still lose points if their paper contains careless errors. No matter how insightful your analysis may be, spelling and grammatical errors will distract your professor from the ideas you are trying to express and you will lose points. Remember that everything you write and submit is a reflection of yourself. You always want to put your best foot forward and submit your best work.

Fourth, read your professor's feedback carefully each and every week. It is surprising how many students do not do so. A good professor will never deduct points without telling you why. Rather than becoming defensive, view an assignment on which you did not do well as an opportunity to learn and improve. Take your professor's suggestions seriously and incorporate them into your next assignment.

Fifth, if you think you are doing everything correctly and are still losing points, contact your professor for guidance. Professors are usually more than willing to speak with you about how you can improve your grade. You need to take this step early in the term so that you can apply what your professor suggests immediately and throughout the class. If you wait until your third or fourth bad grade to reach out to your professor about how to improve your scores, you may risk losing your opportunity to end the class with a high grade.

Sixth, if all else fails, check for errors. In the online environment, both technical and human errors occur. If your professor's feedback indicates that you did stellar work but you still see a point deduction, ask your professor why. It is possible that your professor entered your grade incorrectly or that there is an issue with the grade book. Do not worry about offending your professor—most professors are happy to have such errors brought to their attention so that they can fix the problem.

9.5 I CAN'T THINK OF ANYTHING TO WRITE IN RESPONSE TO THE DISCUSSION QUESTION

It is not uncommon for a student to experience "writer's block" at some point during their educational career or encounter a topic for which they have nothing to say. If this happens to you, do not give up and miss out on valuable points that could be the difference between an A and B.

The source of such trouble is often that the student does not fully understand what is being asked. If you find yourself in this situation, try to write the question in your own words. Check your understanding of the issue with your classmates or your professor. You should also review any responses by your classmates. While you should not assume that your classmates are answering the question correctly, taking the time to review other responses may give you an indication about whether you are on the right track with your understanding of what is being asked. Additionally, if it is possible to respond to a classmate's post while contemplating your answer, you may spur a thread or spark an idea that will inspire you to write your own original response.

From time to time you may also encounter a question for which you feel that the required reading does not give you enough information to answer. If this happens you should perform outside research to gather additional information. Your professor will likely applaud your additional effort, and you may be able to raise ideas that will allow the entire class to see the issue being discussed in a new light. If you go this route, be certain to cite your sources. This is a technique that you can also apply if you registered late for a class and have not yet received the books for the class.

If you are still stumped, you may want to discuss the issue with your friends and family members. While anything you submit to the classroom should be your own work, hearing the perspective of someone not immersed in the topic may provide you with a different perception of the question and provide you with the motivation you need to write your response.

Sometimes the best thing to do is allow yourself some time to let your ideas about a topic fully form. Because your response may be due toward the beginning of each week or unit, you should begin thinking about what you want your response to include on the first day of the unit even if you do not begin writing immediately.

9.6 I NEED TO HEAR FROM MY PROFESSOR AND FAST!

Online students are generally comfortable using e-mail to contact their professors. Many professors prefer communicating with their students via e-mail since they can usually respond quickly. However, keep in mind that many professors are as busy as you with jobs and families. Most are teaching as adjunct professors, meaning they teach part-time, and maintain full-time jobs outside the university. Most professors will respond within 24–48 hours, and many will respond more quickly than that. Your professor's policy regarding responses to e-mail and other forms of communication will likely be posted in the classroom at the beginning of the term. Some professors may respond more quickly than their posted policy states, but you need to be prepared to wait. This means that if your professor states that he or she will respond to e-mails within 48 hours and you have a paper due in 12 hours, you should not wait to hear back from your professor before submitting your paper. Similarly, if your professor has provided you with his or her phone number, you should respect any posted times of availability and not call him or her at midnight even though you are up working on your paper and have an urgent question. A professor is not likely to look kindly on a student who wakes up his or her children with a late-night phone call or calls repeatedly in the middle of a business meeting.

Although most students would like an immediate response, and may feel they need one to complete their work, it is not realistic to expect one. There are some key steps you can take to get the response you are looking for from your professor as fast as possible. In general, keep in mind that your professor needs you to provide all the information necessary to allow him or her to respond quickly.

As obvious as it seems, you should always include your name, course, and section number in all communications with your professor. It is shocking that some students fail to do so, but it happens, especially when students use a device other than a computer to send e-mails. Your professor will not respond if he or she does not know the identity of the person writing.

When sending an e-mail to your professor, you should always include your course name, number, and section. While your professor likely knows your name, he or she may not remember which class you are taking. Making your professor look through all sections he or she is teaching to find your class will waste your professor's time and delay the response.

You should also always include as much specific information as possible. Merely stating that you have a question about "the assignment" does not provide the professor with enough information to give you a meaningful response. You need to specify which assignment and let the professor know exactly how he or she can help you. If you do not understand an assignment, specify which portion of the assignment is giving you trouble. Similarly, if you have a question about a grade, you need to let your professor know your specific concern. Ask a professor to review your "week eight quiz" rather than the quiz you "took last week." If you have a concern about a specific question on the quiz, share that as well. The more information you provide your professor, the faster and more detailed his or her response will be.

If you prefer to discuss something with your professor via telephone, most professors are willing to do so. If you do request a telephone conference with your professor, include not just your telephone number, but specific information about what you would like to discuss. If your professor knows what you would like to discuss ahead of time, he or she may be able to call you very quickly with an answer.

9.7 I AM TOO FAR BEHIND TO CATCH UP

Life sometimes gets in the way. In this book, we provide several suggestions as to how you can best manage your time to avoid falling behind, but despite your best efforts it may happen anyway. Some students simply shrug their shoulders and give up, assuming there is nothing they can do. This is a dangerous approach to take, as even one bad grade can bring down your overall grade point average. Additionally, failing a class can prevent you from moving through a degree program with the rest of your classmates. A failing grade can also have financial aid consequences that may cause problems when you try to register for the next term.

Professors at online schools are usually sensitive to the demands placed upon their students and are generally willing to work with their students to help them succeed. If you find yourself nearing the end of class with much of your work undone, you should first contact your professor and let him or her know why you fell behind and that you are willing to do what it takes to complete missing work and end the class with at least a passing grade. Providing your professor with a concrete plan about how you intend to catch up will demonstrate to your professor that you are serious. In your initial contact with your professor you should include a list of missing assignments and the date on which you intend to submit those assignments.

In order to best position yourself to end a class in which you have fallen behind, you should plan on starting by keeping up with all current work. Then, you should plan on going back and submitting missing assignments with the highest point value first. Although you should submit all missing assignments that your professor is willing to accept, you will see an improvement in your grade faster if you submit a missing 100-point paper before taking a 10-point quiz.

Below is a sample template you can use when you contact your professor.

Missing work and points:
   List each missing assignment and the number of points each assignment is worth.

• Paper:
• Discussion Boards:
• Exams:

Proposed plan to complete missing assignments:
   List each assignment from above with the date by which you plan to submit it.

• Papers:
• Discussion Forums:
• Exams:

Although you should always do your best to finish all coursework by the end of class, if that will not be possible, you should explore the option of obtaining an extension or incomplete. You should contact your professor as soon as you think you will need an extension beyond the end of the term because most schools have strict deadlines for granting incompletes. If you wait until the last day of class, it will probably be too late. You should also consult with your academic advisor about requesting an incomplete, as some schools have policies that prevent you from taking more than one class or moving on to the next level of a given subject while an incomplete is pending.

The most important thing to remember if you find yourself falling behind is that there is usually a way to avoid failing the class or withdrawing as long as you contact your professor as soon as you realize you are in trouble.

9.8 I HAD AN EMERGENCY AND MY WORK IS LATE—I'M SURE MY PROFESSOR WILL UNDERSTAND

As professors we have seen it all—the student whose grandmother passes away (sometimes twice in one year), the soldier unexpectedly sent to Afghanistan, the expectant mother put on bed rest, and the professional laid-off from his job in the middle of the term who is facing foreclosure of his home. No one is immune to these hardships, and we cannot schedule life events to occur at a convenient time.

Many students, however, make the mistake of assuming that their situation is unique and that their professor will be willing to allow them to do whatever they desire under the circumstances. This is rarely the case. As soon as you encounter a situation that you think will prevent you from completing your coursework on time, get in touch with your professor. You should only share the details you are comfortable sharing. When facing a crisis, you should take some time to let your professor know you dealing with an unforeseen situation that may impact your ability to keep up with class. You should also let your professor know when you think you will be able to begin participating in class again and ask your professor if he or she has any suggestions.

You should also be realistic about what your professor can do to help you. One student had a brother who died in a tragic accident in week six of an 8-week class. The professor was willing to accept late assignments from that point forward, but the student tried to convince the professor to accept missing work from the first weeks of class late also. Although the professor had sympathy for the student, the tragedy that occurred late in the term had no bearing on the student's ability to complete work during the first weeks of class. Additionally, bear in mind that as much as your professor might like to help you, his or her actions may be limited by university policies. For example, your professor may want to allow you to submit work after the close of the term, but the university may not allow him or her to do so unless you requested an incomplete before class ended.

9.9 CONCLUDING THOUGHTS

Any number of things can be wrong during the term. Being aware of what can go wrong and what to do if you find yourself in a jam will help you avoid a small problem developing into a much larger problem. As long as you keep the lines of communication open with your professor, you should be able to overcome nearly any obstacle and complete all of your classes successfully.

Opening Doors Through Online Education

CHAPTER 10

Approaching Graduation—Looking for Opportunities

Raquel is in her last term of classes at her online university. She studied healthcare policy and will be graduating in 6 months with a Master of Science degree in healthcare. She hopes to land a job in an administrative position in a hospital near where she lives. She is nervous about how to go about applying, when she should begin looking for a position, and how her degree will help her.

10.1 INTRODUCTION

Raquel, like most students approaching graduation, is anxious about what awaits her once she completes her program. She enrolled in the program to open doors and advance her career. But now that she is nearing the end, she has to make some quick decisions in order to align herself with the right career path. A degree alone is not enough.

While you are enrolled in an educational program, unless you already have a position that you are happy with, you might defer making decisions about a new position or applying for jobs until you are close to graduation or perhaps even longer. This is a mistake and may actually limit your ability to land the job that you want.

When you are enrolled in a degree program, you are dedicated to your studies. You are motivated to complete your degree, which is the reward for the hard work and sacrifice that you made throughout your studies. If you followed the advice in this book, you may have given up things like television, sports, and even fun nights out with your friends for now. You did all of this because you were dedicated to the single goal of getting a degree, which you hope will open doors for you. Good for you. That self-discipline will no doubt move you further toward your goal.

However, once that degree is guaranteed or in your hand, your motivation to continue the high level of work and dedication that you applied during school will drop precipitously. You may breathe a sigh of relief and begin to go back to your old routines, whether that includes visits to the gym, movies, sports, seeing more of your friends, or something else. You will focus less on achieving excellence in your studies and more on enjoying some downtime after so much uptime. This is understandable and you no doubt deserve it for the commitments that you made and kept during school. But this is no time to let your guard down and lose sight of your ultimate goal—a job that pays well in your chosen field.

After a brief period of well-deserved downtime and celebration after you earn your degree, you need to get in the right mindset to look for a new job or position yourself for the promotion that you deserve. Once your degree is conferred, you leave the comfort of school and enter the abyss once again, with no security in a job and no more routine to keep you going from day to day. You no longer have to complete your weekly postings, read your assigned chapters, or prepare research papers. You are on your own. This is a scary place to be.

You can avoid floundering aimlessly after graduation by taking a few critical steps before you graduate and before you start losing motivation. In this chapter, we will address three keys to staying motivated and transitioning seamlessly from a degree-oriented path to a job-oriented path. The three steps we will examine are as follows:

1. Feel out the market at least 6 months prior to graduation.
2. Prepare your résumé and cover letters ahead of time.
3. Aggressively pursue internships and screening interviews.

10.2 ALIGNING YOURSELF WITH THE MARKET

You've decided what kind of a job you would love to have. You've enrolled, and are succeeding in, a program that will prepare you for the career of your dreams. But you have no idea how to actually find that job once you graduate. This is the common downfall of initially motivated students who enter a job market in which they are unfamiliar and inexperienced. And this is precisely why it is crucial to begin your market research as early in your studies as possible.

If you followed the advice in this book before you began your program, you are likely to have already carefully considered the program you chose based upon the available jobs and growth in the field. Presumably, you are in a program that will give you the skills that you require to find entry-level work in this field (or to advance if you are already in the field). However, before you can take full advantage of the skills you are learning, you need to know how to match them to the profession.

To begin this process of "alignment," become familiar with the trade journals in the industry. These may be hard-copy journals, but they are also likely available in online versions. There are likely to be several, although if your field is very specialized, there may be only one or two. These journals could be published by a university, by a trade group, or by other representatives of the industry. Turn to these on at least a weekly basis and begin reading the articles written in your field.

These articles are normally written by experts and are widely read by others in the industry. They will provide you with a basis for understanding not only the latest trends and technology that you will need to succeed; they will also provide you with great interview talking points down the road. It sounds so much better to say, "I was fascinated to learn about the breakthrough research by the X institute, which will really change the direction of this industry," as opposed to, "I remember reading something in one of my classes about that." When you are on top of your game, potential employers will know that you are someone who cares about the business and who will strive for excellence if hired. You will sound like someone who belongs if you read the same articles and use the same lingo as the person who is interviewing you. (Don't forget that many scholarly journals offer student discounts!)

Next, leverage technology by signing up for listservs and blogs related to your field. Start with industry-leading sources to find these lists and blogs, such as through a trade association or similar governing body. These will have the most valuable and valid information for an aspiring member of the field. You don't want to become overwhelmed with information from these lists, so be selective in which ones you subscribe to—read about what information is distributed there before subscribing. With respect to blogs, you should bookmark any that you feel provide substantive insights into the field. Job openings are often posted on listservs, so take special note of those that allow job postings.

A few tips about lists and blogs: (1) don't post to lists or blogs directly unless you have something substantial to offer that is relevant to the readers in general—that is, don't send general requests for employment or questions about how to get started in the field; (2) if you do contact someone from the list or blog, be sure to tell them where you saw their information and ask if they have the time to speak with you—many of these are busy practitioners with little time for their family much less strangers looking for work; and (3) always check the credentials of the people posting to these lists and blogs. Some of them have nothing to do with your field and simply want to share their views on an issue. Those people are not your best sources of reliable information about trends and developments.

Finally, do some online research to get a sense for where representatives from your industry get together. This may be at an annual meeting; via regular training seminars; or some other open forum. If one of these sessions is scheduled to take place near you, and it is not too expensive to attend (note that most meetings also offer student discounts), register and attend the sessions. This is not only a great way for you to stay on top of trends and new research in your field; it is also a great way to network with professionals who already work in the field. If you live in or near a large city, you will undoubtedly find an organized meeting that you can attend to continue your alignment process. Many of these meetings and conferences are held in cities that are also fun destinations. You may be able to combine a graduation trip or mini-vacation with attendance at a professional conference. Given the unparalleled networking opportunities such gatherings offer, there is no better gift you could give yourself.

10.3 PREPARE YOUR JOB SEARCH DOCUMENTS

When the day comes for you to add your new degree to your résumé or curriculum vitae, you will no doubt breathe a sigh of relief. However, even before you obtain your degree, you should be dusting off and shining your résumé and developing cover letters. Rather than reacting to a job opportunity after graduation, think proactively by preparing yourself ahead of time.

Your résumé (called a curriculum vitae or CV for most academic positions) is your calling card. It is a picture of your professional and academic experiences relevant to the job to which you are applying. It should be flexible and tailor-made to every position but that does not mean that you can't begin preparing it before you have a specific employer to send it to. In fact, you may want to prepare a "master résumé" that lays out all of your academic and professional experiences with precise dates and clear accomplishments under each position. You will be able to make changes to your master résumé quickly when you customize it to a variety of different jobs.

Some things to keep in mind when preparing your professional résumé include the following. First, keep it short, but don't sell yourself short. If you have five pages of relevant jobs, consider limiting yourself to only the positions most appropriate for the job to which you want now, those that are most impressive, and those that are most recent. Second, choose fonts and styles carefully. Professional résumés should not be colorful, include scripted fonts, or have icons or other razzle-dazzle on them. Unless your industry is artistic in nature, keep your résumé simple, clean, and professional in appearance. Your qualifications, not your colorful fonts, should be what sets you apart. Finally, be absolutely certain that your résumé contains no typographical or grammatical mistakes. A single mistake can draw the eye of a potential employer and move your résumé from the under-consideration pile to the trash pile.

Once you have a solid résumé ready to go, save it in MS Word format so that you can quickly and easily modify it to distribute to potential employers. You won't have time to proofread it carefully when you are under the gun to get your application out. E-mail yourself a copy (or back it up in the cloud) in case you need it while you are traveling or otherwise away from your computer.

Don't forget to have some cover letters ready also. A good cover letter will attract the attention of an employer by emphasizing the key areas that he or she is looking for in a candidate. Each cover letter should be customized to the particular job for which you plan to apply. But there is plenty you can do in advance to prepare yourself when an opportunity comes along.

Here are some things to keep in mind when preparing your cover letter. First, in almost all cases, do not exceed one page for the letter. Your goal is to quickly attract the attention of the employer, knowing that they are reviewing hundreds of letters just like yours. Second, customize each of your experiences to emphasize skills that broadly apply within the industry. This will make it easier for you to sell your skill set to a multitude of employers. For example, instead of saying, "in this position, I developed a database of clients who I had to call each week to make sure they were satisfied with their services," try "in this position, I acquired database management skills and developed critical customer service experience." Third, remember to include your current or permanent mailing address, e-mail address, and phone number in every cover letter.

If you need help preparing a résumé and cover letters, ask your school's career services office for some samples. Some schools also offer résumé and cover letter review services to students approaching graduation and recent graduates. If your school does not offer this service, there are private review services that may be able to offer you advice for a relatively low cost.

Résumés and cover letters may seem like things you should focus on after you graduate and have a job advertisement in hand. But if you wait until that moment, you will be behind the game and unprepared to face the increasingly competitive marketplace. You *never* want to miss out on an opportunity because you didn't have your résumé and cover letter ready to submit before the application deadline closed. The only way to ensure this does not happen is to be prepared.

10.4 INTERNSHIPS, SCREENING INTERVIEWS, AND INFORMATIONAL INTERVIEWS

10.4.1 Internships

There is no better way to get comfortable within an industry than by working in it. But many employers are unwilling to give you an opportunity unless you bring some experience to the table. So what can you say when your employer asks you about your experience and your only response is, "I took a class on that"?

Internships are a fantastic way for you to acquire the kind of experience that employers are looking for without the commitment of a full-time position. They can open doors to permanent positions with the employer you intern with; they can give you contacts within the industry at other employers; and they can serve as references for you when you apply to the position you ultimately want.

But don't be fooled—internships are both highly coveted and highly competitive in most professional fields. You may be surprised to learn that landing a good internship is often as hard (if not harder) than landing a good job. The process is generally the same as applying for a job—identify an opportunity; make an initial inquiry; customize your résumé and cover letter; and apply—but the salary is less, and internships are often unpaid. The advantage of the internship, however, is that you are able to test out a position without committing to it permanently. You may find that you don't enjoy the work or that it is not what you expected, which ultimately helps you hone your job search to exactly what you desire. Internships also allow you to make key contacts within your field and may give you an advantage over others applying to full-time positions that become available in your industry. If you cannot find a formal internship available, offering to volunteer in an office in exchange for experience and access to those experienced in your field may be a good way to get your foot in the door.

10.4.2 Screening Interviews

Screening interviews are less common than internships; however, they are an even faster way to get a sense of the field in which you plan to work. A screening interview is when you practice your interview skills by meeting with an employer who may or may not be hiring but who is willing to help you develop your interview skills. Your goal in a screening interview is not to land a job but rather to work out the kinks in your interviewing skills before you sit down with an employer with whom you really want to work.

You may do a screening interview with your school's career services office, with an employer who happens to be a friend of the family (regardless of the industry), with an alumni member or colleague already working in the industry, or with a paid service. It is best to do this type of interview with someone you don't know too well so that you can enter the interview with the same level of nerves and stress that you would in a real interview.

When requesting a screening interview, be honest in your intentions. Explain that you are nearing graduation, that you plan to work in their industry, and that you would like to practice your interview skills with someone who is willing to be open and honest with you about your shortcomings in the process. When you do your interview, prepare as you would for a formal interview: dress appropriately; don't be afraid to try out new techniques in the interview; and ask questions about how you did when it is all over. Be open to criticism and take notes on areas in which the employer tells you to improve. They see you through the eyes of your potential employer, so if they see a problem, your potential employer will as well. Be sure to send a professional thank-you note or e-mail once the interview is over.

10.4.3 Informational Interviews

Informational interviews are similar to screening interviews in many respects, but the goal of an informational interview is to obtain information about a field or potential position, not to actually be hired for a particular position. Many employers are willing to sit down with a soon-to-be or recent graduate to discuss their company or opportunities in the field. Alumni of your program working in the field are good potential sources of informational interviews. Because the goal of an information interview is to gather information, it need not be held in person and need not be with someone in your targeted geographical location. Your school's career services office may be able to put you in touch with graduates of your program. If they are not able to do so, you may want to contact former professors working in your chosen field to see if they will meet with you or to see if they can provide you with leads.

Internships, screening interviews, and informational interviews can give you the experience you need to land the job that you want. Completing one or two internships during your studies will expose you to the industry and show future employers that you are aware of what you are getting yourself into. Add to this a number of screening and informational interviews and you will be cool and confident when you sit down with a potential employer—ready to handle whatever they throw at you.

10.5 CONCLUDING THOUGHTS

If you haven't already started any of the things recommended in this chapter and you are approaching graduation fast, don't be discouraged. It is never too late to get started. The more steps you take prior to graduation to prepare yourself for what lies ahead, the further ahead of your competition you will be. As we have reiterated throughout this book, having the degree that you are studying for is a great step in the right direction, but it is one of many steps that you will need to take before you settle in to the job that you want. Be persistent, be aggressive, and remember that the sacrifices you are making now will pay outstanding dividends in the end.

CHAPTER 11

Networking, Leveraging Instructors, and Landing Your Next Position

Maisey studies hard and does well in her classes. She begins a job search and realizes that her high marks are not enough to land a job. She begins to seek out people to help her gather information about how to look for jobs in her field and along the way meets some well-connected people. When one of these contacts hears about a job opening in her office, she calls Maisey, who is quickly called in for an interview and offered the job.

11.1 INTRODUCTION

Education is a journey, not a destination. And while this implies that you should always be learning new things and expanding your skill set, it also means that an education alone is not going to land you a job. Yet, if you are like most of your classmates, your principal goal in enrolling in an online class or program is to find a new job or advance in your current job. You are making an investment of time and money in your program and you expect to get a return on that investment in the form of a job that you want.

A degree alone is not enough to get you the job that you want in most cases. While your degree may allow you to get a raise in your current position (graduate education sometimes qualifies for salary increases in the government, for instance), or may qualify you for a new job altogether, getting the job often requires more than just the degree. You generally need to have experience, contacts, and the right skills for the position beyond the education.

This chapter is meant to help you utilize your time in the online learning environment wisely by preparing you to obtain your next job. You have taken the first step toward getting that job by enrolling in a program that will provide you with the right training. But there is much more that you can do to ensure that your time is not wasted and that you lay the foundation for walking out of the educational institution and into your new position.

11.2 CAPITALIZING ON THE STUDENT BODY

Online education is unique in the fact that it tends to attract a broad variety of students that you might not see on a typical college campus. Traditional schools tend to be occupied by young, recent graduates of high school (or, for graduate programs, recent graduates of college) with little or no experience. In contrast, in online schools, you may find a handful of these students as your colleagues. Instead, you are more likely to find a large group of somewhat older and more experienced students.

The typical online student has taken time off from school to work, raise a family, or both. Accordingly, these students bring with them a wealth of knowledge and experience that you would be wise to take advantage of. On a traditional college campus, you would not gain much insight from the starry-eyed new students; however, in the online learning environment, your opportunity to solicit wisdom, and even contacts, is significantly enhanced as long as you are poised to take advantage of the opportunities before you.[1]

There are a number of reasons why you might want to take advantage of connecting with your classmates in the online classroom. One of them may be working in the field you hope to enter or may have previously worked in a field. You may even find someone who works for the same company that you would like to work for or someone who has friends or contacts that might help you get a job interview. One of your classmates may even be pursuing the same opportunities as you and be willing to exchange ideas and tips for finding success in your field. Failing to be open and interactive with your colleagues may prevent you from taking advantage of potentially valuable contacts, and it may limit your own ability to help others in the process.

Leveraging the online student body to facilitate your own career development, however, is not quite as easy to do as it might be on a traditional college campus. On a traditional campus, you interact frequently outside the classroom in social settings, such as clubs, athletics, and other gatherings. In those instances, you often network inadvertently by learning details about friends and making new acquaintances through small talk. You may not always utilize these

---

[1]See, for example, The Online Student, www.InsideHigherEd.com (July 25, 2012).

contacts right away, but some of them will help you (as you may help some of them) in the future.

In the online environment, you will need to go a bit out of your way to create these interactions, but the same connections can easily be made with a bit of effort. Live interaction is possible with some online colleges and universities, but some are completely virtual. In either case, you cannot afford to pass up the opportunity to network with this experienced and knowledgeable array of classmates. But how do you do that without the opportunity for live interaction?

Below are a few suggestions for making new connections in the online learning environment:

1. Start local by reaching out to colleagues in a class that you are taking. You will get to know your classmates relatively quickly through their postings to discussion forums and interaction in social areas of the classroom. You will learn about their backgrounds through their personal introductions at the start of the course. Pay close attention to those students who live in your area or not too far away. Reach out to them and consider meeting them for coffee or chatting by phone about their interests and goals in the program. I suggest an e-mail like the following:

Dear James,

I really enjoyed your introduction in our Law and Public Policy class. It sounds like you will have a lot to offer in the class as you spent so long working in a prosecutor's office in Miami. I would love to hear more about your experience in that role and perhaps ask you a few questions about how to break into the legal assistant field. I also live in the Miami area and would value an opportunity to buy you a coffee. Do you have any free time in your calendar next week?

Your classmate,

Sarah

A simple and professional message like this accomplishes two important goals. First, it establishes a professional, yet informal relationship between you and your colleague, paving the way for more beneficial interaction than you might get with text messages or comments to the entire class. Second, it gives your classmate an opportunity to bring their experience to the program by sharing their insights with a colleague interested in their work. This flattery goes a long way in opening doors down the road.

2. Utilize technology for long-distance networking. You may not find someone in your class who is living nearby with whom you are interested in speaking. But there may be someone in another state or even overseas that is working in or has experience in your chosen field. Even if you are not interested in moving to another city to find work, this individual may have contacts in your area or may have insights into the application process. Rather than sending them a generic posting in response to their introduction, consider sending them a personal e-mail like this:

Dear Isabella,

I really enjoyed reading your introduction in our Law and Public Policy class. It sounds like you will have a lot to offer in the class as you spent so long working in a prosecutor's office in Miami. I would love to hear more about your experience in that role and perhaps ask you a few questions about how to break into the legal assistant field. Specifically, I am curious as to how you landed your job without any legal training.

I don't live in the Miami area but perhaps we could set up a time to speak by telephone or even Skype, if that is most convenient for you. Are you free to speak next Tuesday night around 6pm your time?

Your classmate,

Sarah

This slightly modified version of the earlier e-mail is a little bit more aggressive, given the geographical distance between you and your colleague. When you are local, it is harder to ignore a request to speak, but when you are miles away, the interest in speaking may decline. Accordingly, propose a time and provide specifics about what you want to speak about. When you do speak, have a list of questions prepared and be respectful of your classmate's time.

3. Start a cohort of colleagues in your field. The first two suggestions above assume that the person you are reaching out to has more experience in your field than you do. But don't limit yourself to vertical networking with those who already have experience; consider

horizontal networking with those who are in the same position as you as well. This means identifying a small group of students that are in similar situations as yourself and forming a group that will exchange ideas, advice, horror stories, and so forth, and that will stay together during and likely after you complete your program. These "cohorts" are often encouraged by online universities to serve as support mechanisms, especially for students in degree programs that have minimal interaction and that instead focus on developing a thesis, for instance. You can rely on the members of your cohort when you need tips on a certain class or professor's expectations, when you want recommendations for selecting paper topics, or even when you just want someone who is in the same boat as you to talk to about your challenges and successes.

Forming a cohort is as simple as finding individuals either in your class or at a live meeting of your program, if you have one. You can always add to your cohort over time and split off into mini-cohorts as you and your colleagues specialize in different areas. To get started, look through your introductory discussion forum or perhaps some substantive forums to get comfortable with your colleagues and to identify those that you believe are in a similar position as you. Then, send them a quick e-mail introduction such as this:

Dear Marsha,

You and I are in the Organizational Management class that started last week. I noticed in your introduction that you have a background in economics and that you are interested in switching from that field to the field of business management. It so happens that I also have a background in economics and plan to move into business management. I would like to get to know you a little better since we will probably be in many of the same classes over the next couple of years. Are you free for an informal phone chat or Skype session over the next week or two?

Your classmate,

Sarah

Of course, this colleague could react in a number of ways—they could ignore you altogether (unlikely); see you as a competitor and keep distance from you; or, more likely, they may be thrilled to have found a companion to walk the long road with, even if you ultimately are competing for work in the same field one day. The chances that you would be applying for the same job are minimal, so the effort is worth the risk.

Build up your cohort over time so that you have at least five close contacts with whom you speak regularly and perhaps as many as twenty with whom you speak occasionally. As all of you in your cohort complete your program and take the next steps to advance your careers, these individuals will make contacts and have experiences that you will not, and they will be much more willing to bring you in on those leads if you are someone they trust and with whom they keep in touch on a regular basis. You will receive priority for any leads they come upon and reject over the cold-call/cold-e-mail job seekers.

As you read these recommendations, you may be thinking to yourself, "I am not the kind of person that just sends e-mails to random people." That is an understandable reaction. It does not always feel comfortable to "target" people in the classroom and send e-mails asking them to do something for us. However, there are three things you should keep in mind here:

1. You will miss a great opportunity to network and potentially multiply exponentially your career development opportunities if you don't network in the classroom.
2. Many of the more experienced students are thrilled to talk about what they've done and lend a hand to those traveling the same road that they traversed years earlier.
3. You will be doing the same for your classmates (see next section).

If you are truly uncomfortable asking someone to speak with you by telephone or Skype, you could ask if it would be all right to e-mail them questions or propose a time to chat via instant messaging. There is no substitute for speaking with someone to establish a strong connection, but some contact is better than none. After a few e-mail or instant messaging exchanges, you may be able to work up to a telephone conversation.

Don't assume that the degree or certificate that you receive at the end of your program is a key that will open a door all by itself. In some instances it may, but you also need experience, knowledge, and a network of outstanding contacts to give yourself the best chance for success. And what better place to begin making those contacts than amongst your peers, who value education as much as you do and who, like you, know the importance of strong networks.

11.3 PAY IT FORWARD

It may not have been the best movie of all time, but the concept is a good one—pay it forward. Think of this as the section on *karma*. You can't expect to follow the advice of the last section successfully if you only take and fail to give. Even in an online learning environment, you can develop a bad reputation. If you are seen by your colleagues as someone who sends relentless e-mails asking for favors but who ignores similar requests made of you, your colleagues will soon turn you away. Moreover, if you are eager to help when you can, those you help will be eager to help you in return. So, learn to give back and you will reap the rewards.

If you are a recent high school or college graduate and you have not yet acquired significant professional experience, you may not have many contacts and valuable information to share at the start of your program. Instead, what you have is energy and motivation to succeed, which is valuable for the older and busier students who may have a hard time keeping up or dedicating the time they need to their work. Offer to help them when they get stuck with technology issues, when they can't find a resource in the classroom, or when they need someone to vent to. You could also offer to take on organizing a study group or compiling class notes into study guides for exams. We suggest two mechanisms for doing this:

- You can easily spot the adult students in the class by reading their introductions. Offer them a kind reply to their introduction (or an e-mail, if you wish) whereby you offer yourself should they get stuck along the way. Your posting or e-mail may look something like this:

Hi Angie,

How wonderful to have someone like you in the class! Thirty years of government service is no small contribution. I am a recent graduate myself, but I have already taken a few online classes and this environment is fairly comfortable for me. Please feel free to reach out to me if you get stuck with the technical aspects of the course, like the navigation tools. I would be happy to help. My email is Sarah@online-school.edu. Good luck in the class!

Your classmate,

Sarah

- Keep an eye on the discussion area where students can post questions and concerns about the course (e.g., the student lounge). If you see a question in there that you can answer, do so. This can be as simple as providing the number for tech support or as in-depth as sharing your take on an assignment. If you are not working, you are probably in the classroom more often than even the professor, so your quick response, assuming it is accurate, can be a major relief for the student that posed the question. Your willingness to help will not go unnoticed and will be greatly appreciated.

As you progress through your program, you will likely take on more advanced classes, and you may engage in internships or begin working in your field before you finish the program. Suddenly you have gone from the inexperienced newbie to the newly minted professional. At this stage, your way of giving back is by making yourself available for younger students that have come into the program after you. These students are energetic and motivated, and it may not be long before they are in a position to help you themselves. If these students reach out to you, perhaps using the same methods you used yourself, respond to them and offer them good advice. Remember that you were in their shoes not too long ago and you want them to have the same access to guidance that you had when you were still finding your way.

As you can see, there is a gold mine of professional contacts all around you in the online learning environment. And again, because of the high percentage of more experienced and working students, the likelihood of you finding valuable guidance and contacts in the online environment may be higher than in a traditional school. So, don't be shy—step right up and start networking!

11.4 LEVERAGING YOUR PROFESSORS

While it is true that a large percentage of your colleagues will have experience and contacts that you can leverage, it is also true that your professors can be valuable resources and contacts for you. Unlike your student contacts, a professor is not likely to refer a job opening to you or mention your name to their professional colleagues. Online (and many traditional) professors often work with hundreds of students over the course of the year, and even those students who stand out and do an excellent job in the class are not on the professor's radar when they return to their practice. But, this doesn't mean that you can't utilize your professors to help you advance your career or that your professor will not be willing to give you advice.

A word of caution before proceeding: Your professor is dedicated to seeing you succeed in your class, in the program, and in your career, but they are also dedicated to your 25 other classmates, the 30 in the other class they are teaching, and their own career outside of teaching. And as you might imagine, these professors—especially the particularly talented ones—receive a number of requests from students for advice on professional development. As a result, they may be less responsive to each request and may have less ability to separate students simply based upon their performance in the class. For instance, it will be difficult for them to identify who would be ideal for a particular job opportunity.

You can learn a lot about your school's professors by reading their biographies in a faculty directory or in the classroom. When you identify a professor whom you believe has the experience that you are working to obtain or the job you would like to one day hold, you need to decide what you hope to gain by speaking with the professor and carefully think about how to best approach him or her. Here are a few examples of what *not* to do in an e-mail to a professor that you want to engage for professional development purposes:

- *Hey prof—I really need your help getting a job. What can I do to get a job like yours?*
- *Prof—do you have any contacts you can give me that might help me find work in this field?*
- *Hi—which classes should I take to help me find a job when I graduate?*

If you get a response from the professor, it will not likely be a helpful one. That is because a professor cannot easily answer these questions and may not think you are taking your professional development and job search seriously. They don't know you personally or professionally outside of the classroom, and these broad questions require some additional knowledge about you and a justification for them to help you. If they respond, they will have a list of questions before they can begin to address your needs. To avoid this, consider an e-mail such as this as an alternative approach:

Dear Dr. Fox,

I am one of your students in CLS1001, Contract Law. I have very much enjoyed your contributions to our class this term—your experience as a private attorney in the contracts field is invaluable for aspiring legal assistants like me. If it wouldn't be too much trouble, may I ask you whether you think a paralegal certificate program like this one will be enough to get a foot in the door at a big law firm like yours, or should I consider applying to law school after I complete this program? I value your guidance and look forward to hearing from you when you have time to respond.

Thank you.

Your student,

Sarah Smith

An e-mail structured in this way makes no assumptions about what the professor is expected to do; however, it also provides great specificity to the request and will allow the professor to respond quickly with the information the student really wants. A professor is much more likely to answer an enquiry like this with valuable guidance, because it is clear what the student is asking and why. If you don't receive a response right away, give it some time. As this is a request outside the scope of the course, the professor may postpone responding until he or she has a free moment. If you don't hear after a week, you might send a brief follow-up message to ensure that the e-mail was received, but don't be pushy. Remember that professors get many of these requests and usually attempt to respond in order and after their regular duties are complete.

11.5 LETTERS OF RECOMMENDATION

In the traditional university setting, it is common for students to request letters of recommendation from their professors to help them secure internships and jobs, apply for grants, and so forth. In those cases, the professor knows the student as a result of seeing them every week in the classroom and possibly around the campus. A student that makes himself or herself known to the professor during the semester with thoughtful participation in the classroom and brief comments following the class to show interest in the lecture are typically students for whom professors are happy to write letters of recommendation at the end of the semester or upon graduation. But what about in the online learning environment?

As we have noted repeatedly, professors have more difficulty getting to know their students in the online learning environment. This can make it harder to justify writing a letter of recommendation for their former students. Remember that a professor who puts his or her name on a letter of recommendation is vouching that the student will perform well in the job or graduate program. If it turns out that the employer wants to speak with the professor about the student, the professor may have very little knowledge to contribute, which can ultimately hurt the student's chances of getting the job.

If your potential employer does not require a letter of recommendation and you simply want to have one on file should you need it, do not request such a letter from your professor. Most professors will not write or sign a blank recommendation—they need to know who it is for and they usually prefer sending it directly themselves.

If you do need a letter of recommendation for a job, graduate program, or some other purpose, consider the following:

1. Try to find contacts that know you well and who can vouch for your professionalism and work quality. Your professor probably can't do this, so look among former employers and others that would be willing to speak on your behalf.
2. If you cannot find an outside contact to write a letter for you and you would like to ask a professor for help, be sure to make yourself known to the professor before making such a request. In order to put yourself in a good position to request a letter of recommendation, you should try to take more than one class with at least a couple of professors and try to distinguish yourself in those classes. If you take only one class with the professor and engage in the classroom to a minimal degree, the professor will not have a chance to

evaluate your work in-depth and you will have a hard time getting a letter out of that professor.

3. Be specific in your request to the professor. Explain which classes you took with him or her, and provide the course name, number, section, and term so that he or she can easily review your work. You should also explain why you need the letter, why you think you are a good fit for the job or program to which you are applying, and why you think that this professor is the best person to write a letter of recommendation for you.

4. Offer to write a draft of the letter for the professor. Most professors receive numerous requests for letters, and we don't always know which qualities we should highlight to help a particular student in a particular job. You may be the best person to write the first draft. Do not put any information in the draft that you do not think your professor would be unwilling to vouch for (e.g., don't add "The student was the best community advocate in his neighborhood").

5. Provide the professor with specific instructions on how to submit the letter of recommendation on your behalf.

6. Remember that you want the process of writing and submitting a letter to be as easy and painless as possible, so give your professor as much information as you can in your initial request.

No matter whom you plan to request a letter of recommendation from, you may want to structure the request as follows:

Dear Prof. Wolf,

As you hopefully recall, I was a student in the recently concluded International Business class with you, BUS 405, Section 03, Fall C Term. We emailed briefly early in the term to clarify the meaning of the Vienna Convention. In your comments on my final paper, you said that I showed "significant promise in the field of international business" and I earned an A in your class. It so happens that I have found an ideal job opening in the field of international business at the International Chamber of Commerce. As part of the application process, the Chamber requires a letter of recommendation. Given your unique knowledge of my skills in this area, I believe that you would be an ideal individual to write such a letter. If you are willing to assist me with this letter, I would be happy to prepare a draft highlighting skills that I believe the Chamber would want to hear about. I can send you that along with the mailing address for you to send the letter directly. I look forward to hearing from you soon, as the deadline for the letter is in 30 days, on January 10th. Thank you!

Sincerely,

Sarah Smith

An e-mail like this is very likely to elicit a positive response and a supportive letter. If you really want the job, find good contacts to write your letters of recommendation and make those requests for letters professional and clear. Once a professor writes you a letter, try not to take advantage by asking for several subsequent letters (one or two is fine). The first letter may be very beneficial, but the fifth may be distant, disconnected, and even negative. So be selective and only request a letter when you really need it.

A letter of recommendation should contain some information regarding your performance in the class(es) taught by the professor writing your recommendation. You should also make your professor aware of any experience you have outside of school that is relevant to the position you are seeking or the academic program to which you are applying for admission.

You may want to structure a recommendation letter that you draft for your professor as follows:

To Whom it May Concern:

I am writing to recommend Melanie Jones.

As her professor in three classes at USA University, I have had an opportunity to observe her participation and interaction in class and to evaluate her knowledge of the subject matter. Her responses were always on-point and thoughtful. I would rate the student's overall performance as excellent.

In my classes Melanie was always eager to accept the challenges of new assignments and welcomed the opportunity to explore the various facets of political science. Her final papers in both courses reflected an unbiased review of the literature and an open-minded approach to the ideas offered. Melanie's research papers were always well written and professional.

I am aware that Melanie is currently employed in the public sector as a paralegal with the US Department of Justice. She has informed me that she aspires to attain a position within a top law firm. I believe she would make a valuable addition to any firm.

Please contact me at (202) 123-4567 if I can be of any further assistance.

Jack Miller, Esq.

Professor, USA University

11.6 WRITING SAMPLE

Throughout this book, we have discussed how to write well. The importance of doing so is not just to excel in class, but also so that you will have a large pool to choose from when applying for jobs or other academic programs. Submitting a well-written writing sample along with your application will give you an edge over other applicants. Any writing sample you send to a potential employer or academic program should be flawless and on a topic relevant to the job or program to which you are applying. You should attach a cover page with a very short explanation of what you are submitting to give the document some context.

A cover sheet should look like the below:

WRITING SAMPLE

Michelle Huggins

2448 19th Street

Washington, DC 20011

Monica_Masters@usaschool.edu

(202) 456-7891

I drafted the attached memorandum on whether the Electoral College should be abolished as a final paper in an upper-level political science class.

11.7 CONCLUDING THOUGHTS

In this chapter, we explained how to leverage your fellow students and professors to help you advance your own professional development. Your unique learning environment means that your networks don't always appear on a campus park bench—you need to seek them out using the technology that the online classroom gives you. When you were last in school, it may not have been that common to engage in virtual introductions and to make friends by e-mailing someone you have never seen before. But just as business contacts today are often formed through virtual introductions, so too can your network of professional development contacts.

When you network with your colleagues, always be willing to give as much (or more) than you are hoping to get. Develop a reputation for being a helper, not an abuser. And when you are networking with your professors, remember to reserve his or her resources for when you are in need of something that your existing contacts cannot give. Be professional, courteous, and specific in your request. You won't be disappointed with the results.

With these tips in mind, you are ready to go out and engage!

CHAPTER 12

Conclusion

Most likely, you bought this book for the same reason that you are considering or have already enrolled in an online educational program—you want to improve yourself and start a better life in a new or more lucrative position. There are many ways to improve yourself, from starting an exercise regimen to learning a new language to volunteering at a homeless shelter. But nothing short of a good education will multiply your growth potential, your earning potential, and your opportunities.

Now that you have completed reading this book and, hopefully, made a decision about your education, you've done the hard part. Sure, picking a school, enrolling, paying tuition, studying for classes, taking tests ... there is a lot still to do. But it is the decision to better yourself through education that is often the hardest to make. Once you make that decision, as you are likely to already know, the rest of the pieces fall into place. You've initiated a momentous process that will continue for the foreseeable future and, hopefully, the rest of your life.

Remember that your education is not only for you. It is for your children, spouse, siblings, nieces and nephews, and even your friends as well. You are setting a positive example for them, showing them the value that you place on education, and allowing them to witness the benefits that your education brings you. You will be a role model and inspire them with your stories of challenge and triumph; encourage them with your tales of struggle and success; and make them envious when you are promoted or hired into a new position based on your educational attainment. Yes, this education is for you—but it is also for them.

When times get tough, remember what a good education can do for yourself and those close to you. Never stop trying to achieve, and always do your best.

So as we draw this book to a close, if there is one piece of advice that we can select from the preceding pages that we want you to pay closest attention to, it is this: Never stop learning. Once you open your mind to higher education, never close it—keep new ideas flowing in and out of your mind every day, whether in a classroom, online, or outside. Your learning experience begins in your household with your family. School strengthens and refines that learning experience to give depth and focus to your knowledge. And the world around you tests your knowledge every day, always pushing you to innovate and problem-solve in new situations. Use this educational opportunity as a springboard into a lifetime of learning experiences. Read more, take more classes, listen more effectively to friends and family, challenge yourself at work, and always push yourself to do better.

With that, we wish you great success in your online studies and tremendous hope for a new future. The road of life ahead may be long and bumpy, but your new education will cushion your journey and make it the best ride you've ever had.

Wishing you much success,

Kevin J. Fandl and Jamie D. Smith

GLOSSARY

COMMON TERMS IN ONLINE EDUCATION

When you begin taking classes online, you will encounter some new terms that may lead to confusion and consternation. Because we also use many of these terms in this book, now is a good time to get familiar with them.

ABD/All But Dissertation Term used to describe a student who has completed all required course-work toward a doctoral degree but who has not yet successfully defended his or her dissertation. Note that a doctoral student may not use the terms Ph.D. or Dr. to refer to themselves prior to successfully defending their dissertation.

Accreditation Accreditation refers to the review and approval process by a national, regional, or state accrediting body of a particular school. The review focuses on the quality of education provided at that institution and its ability to meet the standards set forth by that accrediting body.

American Psychological Association (APA) Scientific and professional organization representing psychology in the United States. Establishes standards for writing scholarly books and articles. APA formatting assistance can be found here: http://owl.english.purdue.edu/owl/.

Asynchronous Asynchronous classes are classes that do not require any live scheduled meetings.

Certificate Program An (often graduate-level) educational program that grants a certificate upon the completion of a set number of courses. For instance, a school may offer a graduate certificate in Art Therapy.

Citation All relevant details about a source used by an author. Citations help to avoid plagiarism and help readers access additional material about a given topic.

Classroom/Courseroom In online education, the classroom or courseroom is usually the web site where the student logs into the class to receive and submit assignments.

Correspondence Education Largely overcome by online schools, correspondence schools offered certificates and degrees to students who received lessons and completed exams via mail.

Course Guide Sometimes used in lieu of a syllabus, a course guide often contains more detailed information about course assignments, grading, and deadlines. *See also Syllabus.*

CV/Curriculum Vitae A detailed listing of an individual's educational and work history, skills, and experience. Usually used to apply for academic positions or grants. *See also Resume.*

Degree Program Unlike a certificate program, a degree program offers a professional degree upon completion of coursework and, if necessary, other assignments. Degrees may include a Bachelor of Science, Bachelor of Arts, Master of Arts, Master of Science, Doctor of Philosophy, and Master of Laws.

Discussion Board/Forum Method used by students and professors to interact in the classroom on a regular basis. In online education, this is meant to replicate the classroom experience that is experienced in traditional education.

Draft A prefinal version of a paper, meaning that it may still require editing and additional research before it is complete.

Dropbox Area of the classroom used to submit assignments in some learning platforms.

eBook An electronic version of a book that a student accesses either via link or download to their computer.

Electronic Databases Online collections of reference materials that can be researched and used as sources in academic papers and essays. Usually accessed through an Online Library.

Feedback Comments that students receive from a professor about their submissions in the classroom. May include a rubric.

Gradebook Area of the classroom where students can see their grades. Most gradebooks show students both their grades for individual assignments and a running total of their grade to date, allowing them to track their progress in the course.

Hybrid University/Program   Traditional universities that offer some classes online and some classes live. Students usually have a choice of whether to take a particular class live or online. Note that some schools also offer live classes that include online elements, such as online discussion forums.

Learning Management System (LMS)   The platform used by an online university to deliver their classes. Common LMSs are BlackBoard, eCollege, Sakai, and Moodle. Note that some schools develop their own LMSs.

Learning Objective   Most schools list specific learning objectives for each class. These objectives outline what a student is expected to learn each week and cumulatively throughout the course.

Live Classes   Classes taught at traditional or hybrid universities in which students physically attend a regular lecture.

Messaging   Some LMSs use a messaging system that is similar to e-mail. This feature allows a student to contact professor and classmates privately using messages rather than via e-mail. Although used in the same way as e-mail, all messages relating to a class stay within the class itself and are accessible via the classroom rather than a general e-mail inbox.

Mission   Many schools employ a specific mission for their existence that is then integrated into the curriculum and learning approach. This may be a particular ethic, religious principle, or other guiding idea.

Online Library   Most online universities offer a web site that provides access to research resources such as online journals, eBooks, and electronic databases. In many cases, they also provide access to a reference librarian who can assist with research efforts.

Online University/Program   An educational program offered completely online that offers either certificates or degrees to students who complete their coursework virtually.

Paraphrase   Summarizing information from another source without directly quoting the original material. Must always include a citation following the paraphrased material.

Plagiarism   Displaying the work of another as if it were your own without proper citation. May include the use of some or all of an original text. Also includes *self-plagiarism*, which is using your own previously published materials in a subsequent text without proper citation.

Points   Assignments may be graded based upon a set number of points. This usually does not change the weight of that assignment in the student's overall grade.

Posts   Submissions made to discussion boards are commonly referred to as posts. Students may be required to submit an "original post" as well as a "follow-up post" or a "response post" to other students.

Professional Journals   Publications by universities and professional associations that present articles and commentary from scholars on particular topics of interest. Often, but not always, peer-reviewed.

Residency   In general, this refers to a particular period of time in which a student is required to be physically present at a university. In some contexts (medical school, for instance), it refers to a specific period of time engaged in practice.

Resume   A detailed listing of an individual's educational and work history, skills, and experience. Usually used to apply for nonacademic jobs. *See also CV.*

Rubric   Rubrics specify how many points will be allotted to specific areas of an assignment. Different points may be given for organization, analysis, use of sources, grammar, and so forth. Rubrics attempt to standardize grading and are often required for major assignments. Some schools also employ a grading rubric for discussion board posts.

Sources/References   Professional or academic articles, books, and web sites that a student reviews and integrates into their assignments.

Study Group   A group of students that choose to work together on a single assignment or throughout a course to facilitate learning and to motivate one another.

Syllabus   Document provided by the professor that lists all readings, assignments, due dates, and grading criteria for a single class. *See also Course Guide.*

Synchronous   Elements of a class that require live interaction. Some classes may require attendance at online live lectures given by a professor given at a set time. These are known as synchronous lectures.

Time Management   Mechanisms employed by a student to effectively balance their schoolwork with other obligations, such as family or work.

Traditional University/Program   An educational program offered completely live with little or no online interaction or assignments.

Unit   Some educational programs divide material into units rather than weeks. This may lead to units stretching across more than 1 week. However, a unit usually refers to a single week. *See also Week.*

Video Seminars   Some online classes employ video lectures recorded by the class professor or another expert on the topic. These are usually accessible asynchronously.

Virtual Office   In online education, a professor maintains a virtual office rather than a physical office, meaning that students can "visit" the professor via chat, e-mail, or phone rather than physically.

Week   Most schools organize work into "weeks." Each school determines what constitutes a week for class purposes. A week may run from Monday to Sunday or may run from Thursday to Wednesday. *See also Unit.*

Weekly Announcements   Announcements posted at least weekly by the professor to introduce the topic, objectives, and important assignments in that week. These should be reviewed carefully by students, as announcements often update or change previously assigned materials.

Wikipedia   This online encyclopedia provides information about a vast number of topics. However, it is not peer-reviewed or carefully checked by scholars and thus the material may be incorrect. Students should utilize this resource for a general overview of a topic and to access a list of additional readings on the topic; however, they should never rely on Wikipedia as a source in their assignments.

Writing Center   Most educational programs offer students access to a writing center where writing experts can provide feedback on nonsubstantive elements of a student's work.